JAC⬛ ⬛ J

D0189161

Routledge Performance Practitioners is a series of introductory guides to the key theatre-makers of the last century. Each volume explains the background to and the work of one of the major influences on twentieth- and twenty-first-century performance.

A leading figure in the development of twentieth century theatre practice, Jacques Copeau pioneered work on actor-training, physical theatre and ensemble acting, and was a key innovator in the movement to de-centralise theatre and culture to the regions. This is the first book to combine:

- an overview of Copeau's life and work
- an analysis of his key ideas
- a detailed commentary of his 1917 production of Molière's late farce *Les Fourberies de Scapin* – the opening performance of his influential New York season
- a series of practical exercises offering an introduction to Copeau's working methods.

As a first step towards critical understanding, and as an initial exploration before going on to further, primary research, **Routledge Performance Practitioners** are unbeatable value for today's student.

Mark Evans is Principal Lecturer and Programme Manager for the degree programmes in Performing Arts at Coventry University.

ROUTLEDGE PERFORMANCE PRACTITIONERS

Series editor: Franc Chamberlain, University College Cork

Routledge Performance Practitioners is an innovative series of introductory handbooks on key figures in twentieth-century performance practice. Each volume focuses on a theatre-maker whose practical and theoretical work has in some way transformed the way we understand theatre and performance. The books are carefully structured to enable the reader to gain a good grasp of the fundamental elements underpinning each practitioner's work. They will provide an inspiring springboard for future study, unpacking and explaining what can initially seem daunting.

The main sections of each book cover:

*   personal biography
*   explanation of key writings
*   description of significant productions
*   reproduction of practical exercises.

Volumes currently available in the series are:

Eugenio Barba by Jane Turner
Augusto Boal by Frances Babbage
Michael Chekhov by Franc Chamberlain
Jacques Copeau by Mark Evans
Anna Halprin by Libby Worth and Helen Poyner
Jacques Lecoq by Simon Murray
Joan Littlewood by Nadine Holdsworth
Vsevolod Meyerhold by Jonathan Pitches
Konstantin Stanislavsky by Bella Merlin
Hijikata Tatsumi and Ohno Kazuo by Sondra Fraleigh and
    Tamah Nakamura

Future volumes will include:

Antonin Artaud	*Rudolf Laban*
Pina Bausch	*Robert Lepage*
Bertolt Brecht	*Ariane Mnouchkine*
Peter Brook	*Lee Strasberg*
Etienne Decroux	*Mary Wigman*
Jerzy Grotowski	*Robert Wilson*

JACQUES
COPEAU

Mark Evans

Routledge
Taylor & Francis Group

LONDON AND NEW YORK

First published 2006
by Routledge
2 Park Square, Milton Park, Abingdon, Oxon OX14 4RN

Simultaneously published in the USA and Canada
by Routledge
270 Madison Ave, New York, NY 10016

*Routledge is an imprint of the Taylor & Francis Group,
an informa business*

Typeset in Perpetua by
Book Now Ltd
Printed and bound in Great Britain by
TJ International Ltd, Padstow, Cornwall

British Library Cataloguing in Publication Data
A catalogue record for this book is available from
the British Library

Library of Congress Cataloging in Publication Data
Evans, Mark, 1957–
Jacques Copeau/Mark Evans.
    p.cm.–(Routledge Performance Practitioners)
Includes bibliographical references and index.
1. Copeau, Jacques, 1879–1949–Criticism and interpretation.
I. Title. II. Series.
PN2638.C74E93 2006
792.02'3092–dc22   2005032857

ISBN10: 0–415–35434–X (hbk)
ISBN10: 0–415–35435–8 (pbk)
ISBN10: 0–203–00100–1 (ebk)

ISBN13: 978–0–415–35434–9 (hbk)
ISBN13: 978–0–415–35435–6 (pbk)
ISBN13: 978–0–203–00100–4 (ebk)

FOR VANESSA

CONTENTS

FIGURES

All figures are sourced from the Bibliothèque nationale de France, and repro-
duced with the kind permission of Mme Catherine Dasté.

ACKNOWLEDGEMENTS

I would like to thank all those who have helped me in the preparation and writing of this book. My thanks must go first to my colleagues and students in the Performing Arts Department at Coventry University. Over the last two years they have put up with regular references to Copeau's work and ideas in almost every context. Their interest and support has been invaluable. It is also impossible to address Copeau's work without acknowledging the eminent scholarship and research which has gone before, in particular that of John Rudlin, Norman Paul, Maurice Kurtz and Barbara Leigh Kusler, whose books and articles have done so much over the years to keep Copeau's legacy alive. Their detailed analyses of Copeau's life, work and teaching offer the interested reader a more wide-ranging resource than is possible here. There is a wealth of material published in French for the student who is confident in the language; I would recommend Copeau's own writings (*Les Registres*) as well as the several biographies available. Unfortunately material on Copeau can be hard to lay hands on, and English translations and articles are not easy to obtain (some key texts are currently out of print). My gratitude goes to the Document Supply Service at the Lanchester Library, Coventry University, for their help in tracking down obscure articles and texts for the purposes of this project. The Research Section at Coventry University provided funds for an invaluable trip to Paris to examine the Copeau archives at the Bibliothèque nationale de France, and to visit the refurbished Théâtre de Vieux-Colombier. My thanks to Simone Drouin and Noelle Guibhert of the Départment des Arts et Spectacles (Bibliothèque nationale de France), and to Éliane Mihailovic (Théâtre de Vieux-Colombier), for their help and assistance before, during and after my visit to France. My thanks also to Catherine Dasté for permission to publish the photographs included in this book, and to the reproductions department of the Bibliothèque nationale de France for providing the images. In addition I am very grateful to Franc Chamberlain and Talia Rodgers for their editorial advice, encouragement and insightful comments during the writing of this book.

Finally I would like to express my deepest thanks to my wife, Vanessa Oakes, for her support and understanding during the writing of this book. It is dedicated to her.

Frontispiece Jacques Copeau on board ship during a visit to New York (1927)

THE LIFE OF
JACQUES COPEAU

In the history of the French theatre there are two periods: before and after Copeau.

(Albert Camus in Saint-Denis 1982: 32)

Jacques Copeau's international success in the fields of journalism, playwriting, directing, acting and teaching represent a level of achievement unmatched in the history of modern French, and perhaps even modern European, theatre. At a time when French theatre was desperately in need of direction and purpose, Copeau, through his writing, his teaching and his practice, offered inspiration and a ceaseless pursuit of quality. His influence on French cultural policy has been profound and his work has also left its mark on the practice and policy of major British and American theatrical institutions. Copeau brought to the theatre of his time a new vitality, purposefulness and energy; an energy based on the actor's physical skills, on a vision of the role of theatre, and on an instinctive feel for the rhythmic and structural demands of a play. In his search for a revitalised theatre – for a theatre which, as in Ancient Greece or Medieval Europe, was able to play a social and moral role with the community – he drew together the influences of other innovators such as Edward Gordon Craig, Adolphe Appia, Emile Jaques-Dalcroze and Konstantin Stanislavsky into a unique and successful synthesis. His innovative work on the use of masks, improvisation, mime and physical expression, as training tools for the actor and as elements within the creation and presentation of performance, have led to his current recognition as a key figure in the history of what is now referred to as 'physical theatre'.

Copeau's influence on the development of twentieth century theatre practice has been diverse and extensive. His commitment to a true ensemble company where actors would play leading roles in one production and minor parts in the next, where the repertoire would include classical revivals and contemporary writing, was a profound influence on the founding principles of the Royal Shakespeare Company in the early 1960s. His belief in the value of a complete and rounded education for the student actor – preparing not just for the theatre of yesterday, but also for the theatre of today and tomorrow – can be seen underpinning the philosophies of many of the leading European and American drama schools. Copeau wrote many articles and pamphlets, but, unlike Konstantin Stanislavsky or Michael Chekhov, he left no handbook outlining his techniques. Though he promoted a broad cultural education for his students, he was equally clear that study through reading was not the way to educate the actor. His legacy has been a practical one; a way of crafting drama handed down by teachers and practitioners, learned through experience and participation. The purity and simplicity of his purpose and his work, his belief in the moral and social power of theatre, and his passionate commitment to the training of the actor's body and mind as well as their voice, have shaped and inspired the work of so many of those who followed after him, both in France and further afield. Much that is now commonplace in contemporary theatre practice can be traced directly back to the work of Copeau and his small group of collaborators during the few decades between the two World Wars. If his influence is not so clearly evident at the start of the twenty-first century, then that is in part because it is so firmly embedded in the cultural framework of the British, European and American theatre industries that it has become taken for granted.

My own introduction to Copeau's work came during my three years as a mime student in London and Paris during the early 1980s. While I grappled with the rigorous and exacting demands of corporeal mime and physical theatre techniques, I found myself curious to discover more about the history and background of the skills that I was acquiring. Copeau's influence has in this sense been a constant presence throughout my career – through my training with Jacques Lecoq, my work in community theatre, and my own teaching. Though Copeau began as a journalist and wrote many pamphlets, articles and lectures, my own experience confirms for me that his theatre methods have been kept alive not only through publication, but also through their dissemination down a line of teachers and students, directors and actors – a living and changing heritage against which his writings need to be seen not as the main text, but as the footnotes, anecdotes and appendices. This book aims to draw attention to Copeau's achievements, practices and ideas so that they may continue to enrich and encourage the practice of new generations of theatre makers.

THE FORMATIVE YEARS

Jacques Copeau was born on 4 February 1879, at 76 rue du Faubourg Saint-Denis in the 10th Arrondissement of Paris. The France in which he grew up was a country of political uncertainty, a country still dealing with the aftermath of the Franco-Prussian War (1870–1871). The war had been a bitter conflict, leading eventually to the end of the Second Empire and the beginning of the Third Republic in France, and the founding of the German Empire. When peace returned to France, it brought with it relative economic prosperity and a growth in cultural activity. Over the following decades France continued to struggle with some profound political and social problems, most notable of which was the notorious Dreyfus affair in which a Jewish soldier was wrongly accused of treason; at the same time, Paris became one of the great cultural capitals of the continent, drawing to it modern artists and writers from all corners of Europe. This social and economic climate enabled middle-class families, such as that of Victor and Hélène Copeau, to prosper and survive, and perhaps encouraged their son's cultural dreams and aspirations. They were a reasonably well off middle class family who owned a small iron factory in Raucourt in the Ardennes, and although they themselves had no notable literary or theatrical connections or background, their son found inspiration in the occasional family trips to performances, the family's small library of melodramas, and from the games and flights of imagination that filled his childhood days. The young Copeau used to imagine the rooftop and courtyard views from his family's house as a stage for his childhood fantasies. His mind, even at that early stage, noting the dramatic potential of the bare architectural spaces – 'like a desert sunrise or a stage after the performance' (Copeau

1990: 5) – and the rich details of everyday activity around him. His childhood passion for games was intense. In his later work, Copeau was often to return to his childhood games and imaginings with a deeply felt sense of their value:

> The mind of a child wanders amid such semblances. He links his own fairyland to the bits of reality that he observes with a relentless eye and absorbs with a bold heart. This is the way we compose our first dramas, which we try out in our games and mull over in silence.
>
> (Copeau 1990: 6)

Copeau was a pupil at the Lycée Condorcet (in the nearby 9th Arrondissement) from 1889 to 1897, during which time he attended various theatre performances at the Théâtre-Libre, the Comédie-Française and the Châtelet: 'I used to sneak out of the house to go and spend the few sous I had carefully saved from my pocket money to attend the theatre' (Copeau 1990: 211). The director **André Antoine** was an important and significant early influence, as he was for many young theatre enthusiasts at the end of the nineteenth century. Copeau was riveted by Antoine's performance in Jules Lemaitre's *L'Age Difficile*, 'Everything he did fascinated me' (ibid.), and, despite the differences in their ideas, Antoine was to prove a friend and supporter of Copeau's work in the years to come.

In his final year at the Lycée, Copeau's first play, *Brouillard du Matin (Morning Fog)*, was performed by his fellow pupils. The young Copeau

---

André Antoine (1858–1943) was a key theatrical reformer and a leading figure in the development of theatrical naturalism. In 1887, with the support of Émile Zola, the novelist and critic who had founded the Naturalist movement in literature, Antoine established the Théâtre Libre. Through his work he stressed the close and scientific observation of everyday life over conventional play construction and hackneyed acting techniques. He later managed both the Théâtre Antoine and the Odéon, retiring after the First World War to concentrate on dramatic criticism. His influence both in France and further abroad was profound, and his support for the next generation of dramatists and theatre-makers was generous and influential.

was enthused by the success of his first experience of making theatre; the fact that it was his own play, put on by himself, must have been important in nurturing his inner belief in the value and power of theatre.

In September 1897 he visited London with his father, seeing the famous English actor-manager Sir Johnston Forbes-Robertson (1853–1937) and the leading actress Mrs Patrick Campbell (1865–1940) in *Hamlet*. On his return he enrolled at the Sorbonne for a degree in literature and philosophy, however he was far more enthusiastic about attending the latest theatre shows than he was about attending his lectures. What money he had he continued to spend on going to performances at the Théâtre Antoine and at the Théâtre de l'Oeuvre, two of the leading avant-garde theatres of the time. Despite failing his written exams at the Sorbonne, Copeau continued with his own writing, completing a one-act play, *La Sève (The Essence)*, and drafting the first outline of his autobiographical play, *La Maison Natale (The Birthplace)*. In June 1901 Copeau's father died; now in his early twenties, he decided to abandon his studies, preferring instead to see the world. He undertook a trip to Scandinavia, including a stay in Denmark where in June 1902 he married a young Danish woman, Agnes Thomsen, whom he had first met in Paris six years earlier. Within the year, Agnes gave birth to their first child, a daughter, Marie-Hélène. Money was inevitably tight, but Copeau managed to support his family by giving private French lessons. At the same time, he continued with his writing, sending several articles to Parisian periodicals. One of these articles caught the eye of its subject, the author **André Gide**, who wrote to Copeau in Copenhagen, encouraging the young writer to continue with his efforts. This correspondence marked the start of a long and warm friendship between the two.

Gide persuaded Copeau to return to Paris with his young family. Copeau's original intention was to continue with his writing, however now that his father had died he was obliged once more to leave Paris –

André Gide (1869–1951) was a French novelist and playwright, whose works explore the tensions between individual hedonism and moral responsibility. His dramatic work included plays as well as translations and adaptations of Shakespeare and Kafka. He received the Nobel Prize for Literature in 1947.

this time to manage the family's iron factory, which he did from 1903 until the business went bankrupt in 1905. His familial loyalty at this important point in his life is an early indicator of his strong sense of moral responsibility and of his personal resolve in the face of fate. As Copeau was ruefully to remark some twenty or so years later: 'From our twentieth or twenty-fifth year on . . . We cease to control our life; it controls us!' (Copeau 1990: 6).

Copeau was now twenty-seven, but according to his friend Gide he looked ten years older; the cares and uncertainties of his twenties had clearly taken their toll. Once again he sought to establish himself in the theatre career he so earnestly desired. Despite his friends' continuing support and encouragement, he complained that he was getting nowhere, 'I do not have the right milieu' (Copeau in Kurtz 1999: 5). Copeau's sense of isolation has to be understood in its context; despite the activities of a few innovators, drama in Paris at this time was dominated by the commercial theatres of the boulevards, and by the artistic and cultural tastes associated with the *belle époque*. He found it difficult to consider how he could work in an art form seemingly so concerned with surface, success, and notoriety at any cost.

The **belle époque** was marked by a taste for all things beautiful and ornate. This period was most particularly associated with the city of Paris between the years 1871 and 1914. Across Europe, scientific and political progress had made for a life that was, on the face of things, comfortable and satisfying – at least for the well-to-do. At its best, this period produced work which was graceful, luxurious to the eye, and enchanting, such as the decorative flourishes of *Art Nouveau*. At its worst, it could produce frivolous and sensational novelty and superficial effect. In the Parisian boulevard theatre of the turn of the century this lead to a system dominated by the egos of star actors and fascinated by the spectacular, the sentimental, the melodramatic and the trivial.

In order to support his family, he turned instead to the world of modern art and, with a recommendation from his friend the painter Albert Besnard, gained work as an exhibition director and salesman at the Georges Petit Gallery. Copeau continued working at the gallery for four years, juggling his work with his writing – doing what he could to champion theatrical reform, and to demand moral integrity and artistic rigour from the critics. In 1907, he was offered the opportunity to take over from Léon Blum as drama critic for the *Grande Revue* – a post which finally gave him access to a wider public. This proved to be an important turning point in Copeau's fortunes, as two years later, Copeau, together with Gide, Jean Schlumberger, André Ruyters and Henri Ghéon, founded the *Nouvelle Revue Française*, which was to become one of the leading French journals of the early twentieth century. Finally Copeau had the financial security he needed to support his family, and more significantly to pursue his own interests in theatre.

Copeau could now start to devote more time to his writing and to his own creative interests. He cut his teeth as a critic by writing for a wide range of journals and newspapers between 1905 and 1913. He was recognised as an important and successful critic – widely read, culturally knowledgeable, perceptive and incisive (Paul 1977: 221). Compared to the polite, anecdotal and descriptive style of most of his contemporaries, Copeau's reviews lambasted the mediocrity and complacency of the Paris boulevard theatres, and repeatedly called to question the extensive commercialisation of the theatre of the time. Underlying his critical writing was a belief in theatre's potential to reveal the true inner dimensions of human life. What Copeau could not bear was the empty theatricality of the commercial theatres, where tricks, traditional stage 'business', hackneyed dialogue and over-simplified ideas of character and motivation brought popular success but revealed little of consequence about the nature of human existence (ibid.: 226).

His first opportunity to put his own head over the parapet came with an invitation from Jacques Rouché to write a play for the 1910–1911 season of the Théâtre des Arts. Copeau chose to adapt and stage Fyodor Dostoyevsky's novel *Les Frères Karamazov (The Brothers Karamazov)*. The production opened on 6 April 1911, and was hailed as a resounding success by the Parisian critics. It was to be revived three times by Copeau during the decade or so that followed. On the heels of this success he was able to visit London and discuss an English revival of *Karamazov* with the actor-manager Herbert Beerbohm Tree, and also to meet the dancer Isadora Duncan. Over the next year, he saw the Ballet Russes perform in Paris, and visited London where he attended a performance of **Harley Granville Barker**'s production of *Twelfth Night* and met with the playwright George Bernard Shaw. Without a doubt the success of *Les Frères Karamazov*, and his subsequent contact with some of the key figures

Harley Granville-Barker (1877–1946) was an English actor, director, critic and playwright. After initial success as an actor, Granville-Barker took out a lease on the Royal Court Theatre in London in 1904, where he produced plays by some of the leading European playwrights of the period: George Bernard Shaw (1856–1950), Henrik Ibsen (1828–1906) and Maurice Maeterlinck (1862–1949). He also produced several of his own plays, as well as ground-breaking productions of Shakespeare's *Twelfth Night* and *The Winter's Tale*. His productions were notable for their lack of declamatory diction, the continuous flow of scenes, the use of open staging, and an emphasis on ensemble performance. In 1923 he moved to Paris, where he began a highly influential series of *Prefaces to Shakespeare* (1927–1948), in which he offered the first comprehensive analysis of the plays from the perspective of the modern actor and director. After working in America during the Second World War, he returned to Paris in 1946, where he died later that year.

of European theatre, was a major factor in Copeau's decision in 1913 to follow his own vision and form a new theatre company.

THE THÉÂTRE DU VIEUX-COLOMBIER (1913–1917)

In starting up his own company, Copeau's ambition was no less than to rebuild the art of theatre from the base up. He proposed a theatre that was 'simple but inventive' (Bradby and Williams 1988: 15), a theatre that would integrate play and performance, with a repertoire based on the classics (principally Shakespeare and Molière) as well as new writing. He intended the emphasis to be on faithful productions, honest and imaginative acting, and minimal stage effects – allowing the poetry and truth of the playwright's work to come through unsullied and pure. In order to achieve this the first and most obvious requirement was a space, and Copeau found what he was looking for in the Théâtre de l'Athénée Saint-Germain, at 21, rue du Vieux-Colombier (the road after which it was to be renamed). The location was far enough away from the boulevards to avoid unwanted competition and comparison, and also sufficiently convenient for his supporters within the intellectual communities of the Left Bank. He saw immediately that the stage and auditorium of the old theatre building would need to be redesigned – eschewing the conventional ornate decoration for a simple, functional stage which would allow direct contact between the actor and the audience. The process of redesigning the new space and of organising

Figure 1.1 Poster for the opening of the Vieux-Colombier Theatre on 15 October 1913

and planning his new company led Copeau into a period of research. He threw himself into correspondence with many of the key figures of European theatre, including Edward Gordon Craig, Konstantin Stanislavsky, Harley Granville-Barker and Adolphe Appia.

He hired a young company of ten actors to form the core of his company. Some were actors he had already worked with, others he interviewed and hired specifically for this new project. In auditioning for the company he looked for indications of the natural and unforced talent and openness that he wanted to bring back to the stage. One young actress, Suzanne Bing, only accepted the salary he offered on condition that she did not have to buy her own costumes – a traditional responsibility of the hired actor, sometimes at considerable expense to themselves. Copeau accepted her conditions, and in an instant he did away with a convention which had financially burdened actors for centuries, and which forced onto the stage a visible reminder of the financial status separating the star and the humble player (Kurtz 1999: 12). Why did these young actors follow a relatively unknown director on such a risky and unconventional venture? Copeau's secret was his ability to inspire others – his vision of what theatre could be and what it could do was passionately felt and eloquently communicated. It was also timely; he appealed to and grasped the imagination and idealism of the young actors of the time, giving their aspirations focus and direction, challenging their creativity in ways that they had probably never experienced before. He intended his new company to work as a disciplined ensemble – a truly innovative theatrical ambition, as, for many years, the pattern of employment had been based around clearly delineated hierarchies in which 'stars' were hired to perform their 'set pieces' alongside companies of jobbing actors. In order to achieve this radical change he realised that he would have to re-educate the young actors who would form the core of his new company. Copeau's primary aim was to free his actor's from the dangers of *cabotinage*.

Though a formal training programme was not an option at this early stage, Copeau decided that he nonetheless needed to take his young actors 'outside the theatre into contact with nature and with life!' (Copeau 1967: 452). The location he chose was Le Limon, a small village in Seine-et-Marne a little over sixty kilometres east of Paris, where he owned a family property. This period of training, rehearsal, discussion and preparation was a nourishing experience for all concerned – bonding the group of actors into an ensemble and helping to establish

---

Cabotinage – Copeau speaks of *cabotinage* as a disease, 'the malady of insincerity, or rather of falseness. He who suffers from it ceases to be authentic, to be human' (Copeau 1990: 253). He used the term to identify the qualities which he most vehemently despised in the commercial actor: the cult of the star performer, the falseness of the 'ham' actor, the use of superficial technique and empty histrionics. It is interesting to note the different emphasis the Russian theatre director Vseveold Meyerhold (1874–1940) gives to the same qualities: 'the cabotin can work miracles with his technical mastery; the cabotin keeps alive the tradition of the true art of acting' (Meyerhold 1981: 122). Though both directors employed a vibrant sense of rhythm, play, comedy and imagination within their work, their differing use of this term indicates key differences between their conceptions of the role of the theatre (see Rudlin 1986: 36–7).

---

a company ethos, shared aims and ambitions. The strict training regime included: swimming, fencing, rhythmical exercises, play-reading, and improvisation; actors were fined for lateness and non-attendance. Copeau also employed open air rehearsals, the simple setting intended to encourage the actors to get used to a lack of technical effects. On a less pragmatic level, he may also have felt that working in the open air in a more rural environment encouraged a different kind of truthfulness and naturalness; in making nature the measure against which his endeavours were compared he was seeking a more profound set of criteria for good acting than those established through nothing more than repetition and tradition. The results were promising, but inevitably limited, prompting Copeau to reflect that it would take 'at least two or three years to get a decent company together' (Copeau in Rudlin 1986: 12). Nonetheless, we can see that from the earliest days of the Vieux-Colombier, training and education were an integral part of Copeau's project, and informed the structure of the company's typical day.

One of Copeau's shortcomings during this period, both as an actor and as a director, was his lack of experience; his ideas outran his practice. He tended to rely on the simple delivery of the text at the expense of discovering its living theatrical expression. At this stage in his career as a director his passion for perfection and precision sometimes left little

Figure 1.2 Members of the Vieux-Colombier company at Le Limon (1913): including, Charles Dullin (seated left), Jacques Copeau (seated at table), Suzanne Bing (seated, second from right), and Louis Jouvet (standing, second from right)

room during rehearsal for the actors' own creative exploration of their roles. His company fondly nicknamed him *le patron*, and indeed, throughout his theatrical life, he tended to find himself drawn to the role of the father-figure, the 'host', the friendly manager, and the 'skipper of the ship'. It needed the polite criticism of one of his young associates, the actor **Charles Dullin**, who had worked with him on *Les Frères Karamazov*, to point out to him that: 'in *listening to actors*, [you] are allowing yourself to be seduced *by the text*, and in your mind [you] are making up for the shortcomings of their interpretation – and therefore not drawing out a full performance' (Dullin in Rudlin 1986: 13). At this stage in the work of the young company it was Dullin and Louis Jouvet who were encouraging a less intellectual and more direct, spontaneous and physical approach; Copeau's confidence in his ideas and in his abilities as a teacher and director was still developing.

Charles Dullin (1885–1949) and **Louis Jouvet** (1887–1951) both joined the Vieux-Colombier in its early years. Dullin eventually left to form his own company in 1919. He later established himself as a key figure in French theatre through his work at the Théâtre de l'Atelier as an actor, director and teacher. Jouvet, who had performed in *Les Frères Karamazov (The Brothers Karamazov)*, joined the Vieux-Colombier as stage manager (regisseur). He left Copeau in 1922 in order to form his own company, and, like Dullin, he enjoyed considerable success in his own right. They were both members of the Cartel des Quatres ('Group of Four'), which dominated Parisian theatre after the First World War, and shared in the directorship of the Comédie-Française for a short period.

The Théâtre du Vieux-Colombier announced its opening to the people of Paris with a bold and simple poster proclaiming its aims and ambitions and calling on the young and cultured of the city for support (see Figure 1.1). It opened its doors to the public on October 22, 1913, with *Une Femme Tuée Par La Douceur* (*A Woman Killed With Kindness*) by Thomas Heywood and *L'Amour Médecin* by Molière. The new company's subsequent repertoire combined classical plays and new writing in equal measure and was met with interest and enthusiasm by the serious theatregoers of Paris. Though Copeau sometimes struggled to achieve the fluidity of expression to which he aspired as a director, nonetheless the freshness and vitality of his productions shone through. The young company was obliged to forge its identity within the crucible of its public performances; but the benefit was an inner collective strength and a subtle understanding of each other's acting that was to produce, at the very end of the season, a success which justified all his efforts and made Copeau confident of the route he now wished to take.

The company's first major success, *La Nuit des Rois (Twelfth Night)* by William Shakespeare, opened on 19 May 1914 to almost immediate critical acclaim. By the opening night the company were exhausted – Copeau and Jouvet had been up all night organising the lighting, and the costume designs were finished as the actors prepared to go on stage and perform. Copeau's single-minded dedication to simplicity, sincerity and detail, coupled with the bonding experience of the limited training spell in the country and a season's experience of collaboration, produced fine ensemble playing and high performance standards. The risk had finally paid off. So successful was Copeau's lyrical, comical and inventive inter-pretation of Shakespeare's play, that the company received numerous invitations to tour. In late summer 1914 preparations for touring and for the next season were well underway when war was declared; suddenly fate had swung against Copeau – he and his actors were dispatched to the Front and his theatre was requisitioned as 'a shelter for refugees and soldiers on leave' (Kurtz 1999: 32).

COPEAU AND CRAIG

> There has not been a single artist of the theatre during the last twenty-five years who is not indebted to a greater or lesser extent to Gordon Craig.
>
> (Copeau 1990: 14)

Copeau had heard of Craig's work and was a subscriber to Craig's influential journal, *The Mask*. He had asked Craig for permission to publish some of his writings and designs in the *Nouvelle Revue Française* (Bablet 1981: 183), and subsequent correspondence between the two men confirmed their shared views on theatre and the Arts. When he was invalided out of the French auxiliary forces in April 1915, Copeau decided to make use of his time by visiting those people whose work he saw as complementary to his own ideas and aspirations. His first visit was to **Edward Gordon Craig**'s school in Florence during the autumn of 1915.

It was this meeting which helped to convince Copeau of the importance of training new actors, of 'welcoming the young', for a rejuvenated theatre. Craig's aim was to provide within his school an environment that enabled and encouraged creative experimentation. Both Craig and Copeau agreed on the importance of developing a high level of technical skill:

> It is neither talent nor ideas that are lacking, nor heart, nor need. It is the discipline of craft which once reigned over even the most humble endeavor. It is the rule that to think well leads to the ability to do well, competency with perfection in mind. Art and craft are not two separate entities.
>
> (Copeau in Felner 1985: 37)

Furthermore, both believed in the value of study programmes that encouraged the student to acquire a full and rich understanding of the wider cultural environment.

Copeau shared Craig's recognition of the important role of the director and designer in the creation of a new artistic vision for the theatre; where he differed with Craig was over the role of the actor within this vision. While Craig's disenchantment with conventional acting led him towards reconfigurations of the actor as a kind of marionette to the will of the director, Copeau was convinced that the actor must remain a central part of the theatre event and its creation. On the other hand, Craig's vision of a stage stripped of the fussy decorative naturalism of the nineteenth century and his ideas for creating atmospheric spaces within which theatre could generate a new synthesis of scenic movement and *mise-en-scene*, provided Copeau with affirmation for his own idea of a *tréteau nu* on which the actor could (re)create a poetics of theatrical expression. Having looked at Craig's designs and discussed with him the use of screens and the principle of the single scene, Copeau was enthused enough to write to Jouvet: 'it is exactly what we need for our stage ... One might be able to improve a few details in the course of working with this material, but as it stands, it satisfies *all our needs*' (Copeau in Bablet 1981: 184). Craig also showed Copeau an idea for a stage lighting scheme that avoided the contemporary fashion for footlights and battens. All these ideas came together in Copeau's imagination, building a realisable image of a theatre which, incorporating permanent stage architecture, use of levels and steps, could finally achieve 'an unbroken transition from auditorium to stage' (Bablet 1981: 185).

By the time Copeau had to leave Craig and return to France, he had arrived at his own assessment of Craig's ideas. While he valued Craig's flashes of insight, vision and erudition, which could be both illuminating and inspiring, he also recognised the lack of clear direction which could make Craig's work sometimes seem to be 'so useless and almost puerile' (Copeau 1990: 17). Copeau's comments betray a frustration with Craig's idealism; he believed that Craig was wrong to avoid the necessity to *realise* a new theatre, not merely to dream of it. How could any 'movement for the renewal of dramatic art which is not accompanied or necessitated by the production of new work' possibly be 'realistic, living, necessary' (ibid.: 18)? Furthermore, whereas Craig saw the theatrical event in terms of staging, design and lighting, Copeau sought to achieve his effects through the actor's 'gracefulness, his airs, his acting and delivery' (ibid.: 19). As Craig himself admitted to Copeau, 'You believe in the actor. *I do not*' (ibid.: 22). Copeau was to continue his journey of study and reflection deeply inspired, greatly excited, certain of his own route, and also convinced that: 'there is infinitely more soul and a more fertile seed-bed in my little theatre, which exists and lives with all of its poverty and imperfections' (ibid.: 19–20).

COPEAU, JAQUES-DALCROZE AND APPIA

In 1915 Copeau had acquired a short pamphlet on the work of **Emile Jaques-Dalcroze** (Jaques-Dalcroze 1913). Inspired by Jaques-Dalcroze's work, Copeau willingly accepted a government invitation to spend a short period in Geneva as a cultural ambassador for France during the summer of 1916, as this meant that he was able to visit Jaques-Dalcroze's school regularly and to watch Eurhythmic classes (Copeau 1990: 59–62). He took with him his daughter, Marie-Hélène, and a member of his company, Suzanne Bing, both of whom were to become invaluable and committed associates in his future work.

Emile Jaques-Dalcroze (1865–1950) was an unlikely figurehead for the development of early twentieth century movement and dance. A portly and dapper composer and music teacher, he had begun his work on movement in order to find a method to release his music students' natural understanding of rhythm. In adding rhythm to gymnastic education, Jaques-Dalcroze emphasised the dynamic qualities of the body over the static, regimented practices of the previous century. For him, rhythm was a universal and essential component to all expression. After being dismissed from his post as Professor of Harmony at the Geneva Conservatoire he continued to teach, founding his own school. His movement work was quickly recognised as a pleasurable and liberating alternative to the functional, mechanical exercise of traditional drill and the rigidly formal vocabulary of the ballet, offering instead a unified and expressive approach which could be adapted to several potential uses.

Copeau shared with Jaques-Dalcroze a passionate interest in exploring how the mental and physical facilities of the performer could be developed to the point where 'the muscles would do the will of the mind easily and quickly' (Spector 1990: 56–7). He had a deep respect for Jaques-Dalcroze's empirical approach, the way that he worked from experience, through improvisation and experiment, encouraging his students to reflect constantly on the emotional effect of their practice (Copeau 1990: 60). The entire body and person of the performer might in this way be unified in theatrical expression, precisely the effect that Copeau wanted his young actors to achieve.

He was impressed enough with Jaques-Dalcroze's work to try a few experiments of his own in Paris, and later to invite a young student of Jaques-Dalcroze, Jessmin Howarth, to work as movement teacher with his company. Miss Howarth was to travel with the company to New York in 1917 and reportedly 'not only drilled the troupe regularly each day in rhythmic gymnastics but also observed each rehearsal' (Rogers 1966: 178–9). The experiment did not work; Miss Howarth, and a later replacement, Jane Erb, were both dismissed by Copeau. Despite such problems, Copeau and Jaques-Dalcroze shared a life-long admiration for each other's work, each recognising in the other a fascination with the interaction of rhythm and movement in the work of the actor and performer.

Whilst in Switzerland, Copeau also took the opportunity to visit the designer **Adolphe Appia**, who had collaborated with Jaques-Dalcroze in setting up the innovative training establishment for Eurhythmics at Hellerau, in Germany.

Adolphe Appia (1862–1925) had been inspired in his youth by the work of the composer Richard Wagner, in whose compositions he saw a vision of a theatre of the future. His innovation was to set aside the traditional conventions of staging and work solely from the inner qualities of the music or text itself. He rejected pictorial staging and focussed instead on the three dimensional dynamics of people moving in space. To this end he proposed a simple space, using movement, lights and stage levels to create his effects. In 1906, Appia attended a demonstration of 'Eurhythmics' by Jaques-Dalcroze and his students. Jaques-Dalcroze's work offered a way in which the actor's body could take its central place as a carrier of the action without breaking the rhythmic spell of the music. Appia began a collaboration with Jaques-Dalcroze which was to last through various projects and productions, including the influential school of Eurhythmics at Hellerau in Germany, until Appia's death in 1928.

Copeau called Appia his 'master' (Hayman 1977: 86), and shared with him a belief in the primacy of the actor within the theatrical event. Copeau remained in contact with Craig, Appia and Jaques-Dalcroze throughout his life, and his debt to their pioneering work is clear. His conversations with all three confirmed his conviction that the conventional hierarchy of the nineteenth century stage – spectacle, music and effect over the spoken word, the rhythms of the text and the scenic interplay of the actor and space – should be challenged and changed. Copeau had the insight, the theatrical experience and the working environment in which to resolve the problems such innovations posed. In an important sense, Copeau was the conduit through which the idealistic visions of Craig and Appia could find theatrical realisation. As Copeau himself was to write to Appia:

> What shocks me, and worries me, is that you and Craig, you are building the theatre of the future without knowing who will live there, what kind of artist you will put on the stage, or house in the very theatre you wish to welcome them. It seems to me, Appia, that I alone have begun at the beginning in taking on the job of forming a troupe of actors.

(Copeau in Folner 1986: 30)

THE VIEUX-COLOMBIER IN NEW YORK (1917–1919)

In January 1917, Copeau was again dispatched as a cultural ambassador by the French Ministry of Fine Arts. This time he was sent to the United States as part of a drive by the French Government to encourage American involvement in the First World War – a task made all the more urgent by the terrible events on the battlefields of France, where several of his first company had already fallen. His lectures were an unusual success, given that they presented a profound critique of the dominant commercial theatre in America. The lecture tour resulted in a lively interest in the work of the Vieux-Colombier Theatre, and an invitation was made to bring his troupe to New York, with financial support from the wealthy banker and philanthropist Otto Khan, who was eager to help introduce the new European stagecraft to American audiences. There were difficulties to overcome, it would mean bringing together a troupe of performers that had been disbanded for several years; identifying a suitable venue; and, less attractive to Copeau, the manipulation of the troupe's repertoire to suit American tastes and interests. The tour was an inherently risky venture. Several months of planning and organisation had to take place, including the search for and

Figure 1.3
The courtyard in
which Copeau
established the
Vieux-Colombier
School in 1920

redesign of a suitable New York theatre. However Copeau succeeded in gathering together almost all of his pre-War company, and his previous theatrical success also allowing him to recruit several talented new actors. The season opened at the Garrick Theatre in New York on 27 November 1917 with a performance of Molière's late farce, *Les Fourberies de Scapin*. The success of this and other productions speaks volumes for the young company's ability to overcome the problems of language and culture. This was in no small part a result of the emphasis Copeau placed on simple staging and expressive physical movement. As a director he was learning to pay careful attention to the rhythm of the text, its dramatic choreography and poetry. His New York revival of *Les Frères Karamazov (The Brothers Karamazov)* also demonstrated an increasingly confident grasp of psychological characterisation. Copeau's knowledge of Stanislavsky's techniques for psychological realism was, of course, limited, and it was to be another six years before the visit of Stanislavsky and the Moscow Art Theatre to New York, however his intuitive understanding of the need for sincerity and truth on stage enabled him and his company to achieve some success in this respect. It is a mark of the achievement of Copeau's young company that the programme for the New York season could proudly announce that:

> The Théâtre du Vieux-Colombier is the youngest of French theatres, and the only one which can be compared to those numerous artistic stages that have been created abroad during these last twenty-five years.
>
> (from 'French Théâtre du Vieux-Colombier', programme for New York season, 1917–1918, Fonds Copeau, Bibliothèque nationale de France, p. 3)

Both the lecture series and the New York tour served their purpose in generating interest in French culture, but they also had a significant influence on the development of the American **Little Theaters**.

The Little Theater movement found inspiration in Copeau's commitment to effective dramatic expression, the work of native playwrights, a rejection of the commercial theatre system, and to creating and building an audience sympathetic to the work (Kurtz 1999: 48). The Vieux-Colombier's visit to New York thus played a vital role in re-establishing the international importance of French theatre. Nonetheless, despite this recognition, Copeau's intentions were more straightforwardly to nurture and protect the integrity of the Vieux-Colombier Theatre's mission. The New York season was actually important to Copeau

---

The **Little Theater movement** began in America around the second decade of the twentieth century. The movement arose as a response by the cultured middle classes to the popular success of the early cinema and to the perceived irrelevance of the commercial theatre to contemporary issues. Its members sought to promote 'serious' theatre, putting on their plays in community venues and small, intimate performance spaces, rejecting detailed naturalistic staging, experimenting with form, and encouraging new writing. The movement was also closely associated with the development of drama studies in American universities and colleges.

---

because it gave him an opportunity to explore in more depth and detail the ideas gleaned from his visits to Craig, Jaques-Dalcroze and Appia, and through his correspondence with Stanislavsky.

His success in America, while significant, was only partial. The audiences were selective in their taste and he was forced to compromise with his programming in order to ensure an adequate degree of box office success. The conditions of his tour and the nature of his financial backing meant that he was reliant on a society audience who were not naturally in tune with his ideas and ideals. A proportion of the audience and critics seemed to have expected something more rich, elaborate and ornate, something more star-studded and flamboyant, than the typically simple and uncluttered productions which Copeau had delivered. But over the duration of the tour, as a result of sticking to some of his plans and compromising on others, Copeau's work had begun to find regular followers and friends. Nonetheless, Copeau's work load during the tour was gruelling – between November 1917 and March 1919 he produced 44 different plays (Harrop 1971: 115–16). Eventually, the stress of such an extensive and demanding schedule took its toll on the actors' energies, and Copeau became aware that not all his actors were able or willing to explore the new challenges he wished to confront. Company cohesion started to suffer. Despite the overall sense of success, and despite the strong friendships and associations he had made, it must have been a sweet relief for Copeau eventually to return to Paris and to resume his own creative mission once more.

THE COMPANY RETURNS AND THE SCHOOL RE-OPENS (1919–1924)

By 1919, Copeau's international success as a director of both classical revivals and modern plays meant that he had become established as a leading figure in French and world theatre. However, this success and recognition was not enough to lift the Vieux-Colombier out of financial danger. In part this was because the theatre could only hold 363 people – minute in comparison to the cavernous capacity of the major boulevard theatres – but Copeau was resolutely against any form of financial support (government or private) which might, as he saw it, bind him to another's agenda: 'I don't want state funds, they would choke me' (Copeau in Kurtz 1999: 69). It is fascinating for us today that such a distinctive and rigorous theatre experiment could occur on such a scale, with virtually no state support, relying almost entirely on private finance, box office income and patronage. For Copeau, meaningful experiment could not happen without freedom from outside interference, nor away from the support of a loyal public:

> The Vieux-Colombier is not a fantasy of amateurs or intellectuals concocted to tickle the curiosity of snobs and to win for itself the ephemeral favor (sic) of great philanthropists. It is a work of slow construction, open to all workers of the theatre, and destined for the general public which must give it life.
>
> (ibid.: 70)

Copeau chose to open the company's new Paris season in February 1920 with a production of *Le Conte d'Hiver (The Winter's Tale)*, adapted from Shakespeare by Copeau himself and Suzanne Bing – a story of rebirth and forgiveness, appropriate for a country recovering from the ravages of a long war. However, the surprise hit of the season was to be his production of Charles Vidrac's play *Le Paquebot Tenacity*. This play was full of naïve charm, staged with simplicity and sensitivity, preferring understatement and subtlety to the overblown acting of the boulevards. The uncluttered, poetical realism of these productions set out clearly the guiding principles of Copeau's directorial style.

Buoyed by the recent critical acclaim, and encouraged by the support of friends and enthusiasts through Les Amis du Vieux-Colombier (The Friends of the Vieux-Colombier), Copeau now entered into a period of well-earned professional success and intense theatrical activity. During the first season before the War, less than one-sixth of the Vieux-Colombier's performances had been of new work – now, during the 1920 season, nearly half of the plays Copeau produced were new works (Kurtz 1999: 68). This change in emphasis marked a real turning point for Copeau's original mission – the rejuvenation of French theatre could not take place solely through a return to the classics, the lessons learnt from the past must be brought to the service of the theatre of today. The Vieux-Colombier, through its successes, had become the fashionable place to go, and new playwrights strove to get their plays put on there. Copeau's theatre offered an environment that welcomed playwrights as a key creative force within the theatre; he encouraged writers to explore the 'poetic' possibilities of drama as a medium, and crucially offered them the theatre resources to do so. Writers such as Georges Duhamel (1884–1966), Jules Romains (1885–1972), and Charles Vildrac (1882–1971) responded willingly to this opportunity and began the re-invigoration of theatre writing which was to place French drama at the heart of European theatre over the next four decades.

At last Copeau felt able to restart the Vieux-Colombier School. His initial attempts in 1913, and again in 1915, to provide a training regime for the actor had been stalled as a result of the outbreak of war. He had always intended that a school for actors would be the foundation stone of his project to rejuvenate the theatre. He knew that despite his own and his company's success, more work needed to be done in order to develop a genuinely spontaneous, sincere and vital theatre. While his dream of establishing a school that would run alongside the theatre company was not entirely innovative – other schools for actors had already opened their doors across Europe (e.g. Beerbohm Tree's Academy of Dramatic Art in London and Stanislavsky's Studio in Moscow) – nonetheless Copeau's school offered a new and serious challenge to the dominance of the Conservatoire Nationale de la Musique et d'Art Dramatique as the principal centre for actor training in France. The Conservatoire primarily drilled students, through the most pedantic and functional of training regimes, to become actors of set roles with the Comédie-Française – what Copeau offered was, in comparison, nothing short of revolutionary in its focus on creativity, spontaneity and physicality.

THE VIEUX-COLOMBIER SCHOOL (1920–1924)

The School opened its doors once more in February 1920, the first year intended as a pilot enterprise involving a limited number of students.

The first classes were held in a barn in the Theatre's courtyard, but this space proved too cramped and the School soon moved a short distance away to better facilities at 9, rue du Cherche-Midi. Difficult experiences with some actors during the New York tour meant that Copeau had become convinced that the future lay with training children rather than re-educating actors who had already been formed by what he saw as a corrupting system: 'the only hope we can have in the future of the theatre is . . . the training of children' (Copeau in Kusler 1979: 20). The first classes therefore focussed on teaching the young group voice technique, simple characterisation and group performance. This work laid the foundation stones for the more ambitious plans for the school in the following year.

The inclusion of classes for children was important; Copeau did not want the school to be restricted to training actors for the company. Instead he aimed to provide within the School a space for exploration and experiment, as well as for the public dissemination of his ideas. Copeau had always aimed to open a school before starting a theatre company, but initially he felt that he had 'neither the authority nor the means to do so' (Copeau 1990: 28). He realised the impossibility of managing the School alongside all his other responsibilities, and asked the philosopher, novelist, playwright and poet Jules Romains (1885–1972) to be Director of the School. Romains was, by inclination and belief, as committed as Copeau to the idea of developing a community of actor-artists. For Copeau inclusion of the School brought his whole enterprise closer to the great models of the past, the theatrical 'families' of the commedia dell'arte troupes and the great Japanese Nōh companies, in which training, living and performing became part of an indistinguishable blend of activity.

The legacy of the visit to New York was evident through some important developments within the company, which now did much to shape this next phase in Copeau's work. The actress **Suzanne Bing** had become increasingly involved with the teaching of student actors. Whilst in New York, she had visited schools and observed children's games and play; this led to a fascination with improvisation, animal mimicry, games and the basic skills of what was later to become modern mime. Working closely with Copeau, she developed these elements as key features of the teaching and training at the Vieux-Colombier School. During this period, Bing was to become the key figure in the day-to-day work of the school. She had a close understanding of Copeau's aims and her commitment to the development and success of the School was such that she was prepared to give up acting with the company in order to make it happen: 'It was necessary that I chose between the theatre and the school' (Suzanne Bing in Mignon 1993: 204, author's translation).

Suzanne Bing (1887–1967) was a leading actress and teacher at the Vieux-Colombier, with Les Copiaus and later with the Compagnie des Quinze. She married the composer Edgar Varèse (1883–1965) in 1906, moving with him to Berlin in 1907. In 1913 she and her husband divorced, she had trained at the Conservatoire d'Art dramatique and it was to the Paris theatre that she now returned, joining the Vieux-Colombier Theatre in its first season. She had an affair with Copeau, with whom she had a son, Bernard Bing, born in 1917. She became one of Copeau's closest associates; she was a key member of the teaching staff at the Vieux-Colombier School and later a leading member of Les Copiaus. Her teaching was influential in the development of modern mime and mask improvisation techniques, and of physical training for actors.

At the same time, Jessmin Howarth's attempts to train the actors in the basics of Eurhythmics had proved less than successful, perhaps her inexperience had been at fault but the result was that her classes had been poorly attended. Copeau had also become increasingly disillusioned with Eurhythmics, which he found prone to artificiality and self-consciousness: 'It cannot be directly applied to our training. It already bears within itself an affectation' (Copeau in Kusler 1979: 18). After Howarth's departure, her teaching input was split between dance classes, the 'natural gymnastics' of **George Hébert**, and movement improvisations led by Bing.

Suzanne Bing had taken notes on Howarth's movement classes, focusing on aspects of interest to her (silent pantomime, sensory experience, the essential rhythms of characters) which she was now able to integrate into her own teaching. In synthesising these influences, Bing was a crucial contributor to Copeau's efforts, helping to draw together his many ideas and principles into a coherent method of actor training. Copeau's frequent and prolonged lecture tours, and his work as a director and actor with the Vieux-Colombier company, meant that Bing's teaching was effectively the heart and core of the work at the

George Hébert (1875–1957) was a significant influence on the development of physical education in France. After a career as a naval officer, during which he noted with fascination the natural fitness, strength and flexibility of the 'button boys' who climbed the rigging of the tall ships, he travelled extensively, observing the physical prowess of indigenous peoples who had not had any form of formal gymnastic training. Later, as a teacher of physical education at the College of Rheims, he formulated his own theories and principles based on the 'natural' practices he had observed and on Ancient Greek physical ideals. His system rejected the mechanical repetition of the dominant Swedish method, and proposed that physical education should be linked to an observation of and interaction with Nature. Hébert sought physical development through 'organic resistance, muscularity and speed', basing all exercise around walking, running, jumping, crawling, climbing, balancing, throwing, lifting, swimming and self-defence. He was an early advocate of exercise for women. His influence can be seen in the development of obstacle course training, the physical theatre training of Jacques Lecoq (Murray 2003: 30), and even in the contemporary urban extreme-sport of 'free-running' or *parkour*.

School. Copeau's close personal relationship with Bing meant that he was always in touch with the developments at the School, and he liased frequently on the students' progress. Suzanne Bing has not generally been credited for the significant contribution she made to the School; to her fell the task of testing many of Copeau's pedagogical ideas through practice, and through her teaching she was to develop much of the detail of corporeal mime technique and mask improvisation.

For Copeau, the first and most important task of the school was to rediscover the rules of theatre. This was to be achieved through the complementary activities of experiment (using improvisation and physical technique), and of historical research (in particular into the theatrical traditions of Ancient Greece, the Middle Ages and the Renaissance). The resulting programme of study indicates Copeau's determination that his students should see their training as the preparation of an artist, not the drilling of a journeyman. They were to become, 'interpreters of dramatic forms whose realisation we have as yet not been able to imagine for lack of a proper instrument' (Copeau in Kusler 1979: 20). The next three years of the school represented the most complete expression of Copeau's work on the training of the actor. The newly expanded programme of training, which began when the School opened in its most complete form in 1921, included three strands which represented the main aims of the school: courses for the general public; courses for student actors and other theatre artists; and courses for young people and children without previous acting experience. Of these strands, by far the most important to Copeau was the last – it was in this group of apprentice actors, untainted by the bad habits which he saw as endemic in the profession, that he saw the possibility for a theatre art of the future. The apprentice group started in 1921 as a small class of six students, at the core of which were several pupils, including his own daughter Marie-Hélène, who were to stay with Copeau's project for the rest of the decade. It was with this young group that Copeau and Bing felt able to make their most profound experiments in actor-training; it was in their classes that Copeau first introduced the mask as a training device. And it was this apprentice group, directed by Suzanne Bing, that produced a revival of the classical Japanese Nōh play, *Kantan*, that, for those who saw it, marked the highpoint of the School's achievement. The mix of family, friends and newcomers, the atmosphere of experiment and playful innovation, helped to foster the spirit of a company and school linked by connections which went deeper than professional and commercial need.

The work of the school was so new and innovative, that there were few markers for Copeau, Bing and the other teachers to follow other than their own instincts and experience, and Copeau's knowledge of developments elsewhere in Europe. Inevitably, as one of his students noted, 'discovery became the common task of master and student' (Michel Saint-Denis in Kusler 1979: 30), with Copeau counting on his students to help him move the work forward. The enthusiasm of the students was high, the atmosphere a heady mix of invention, discovery, liberty and discipline. Enthused by the success of the School, Copeau re-organised the whole enterprise, moving his colleague Jules Romains to oversee the expanded public course provision (and eventually removing him altogether from the School), so that Copeau could take more active charge himself.

COPEAU AND STANISLAVSKY

Just as he had found inspiration in the staging concepts of Craig and Appia, Copeau now found another mentor who could provide an equally compelling vision of the art of the actor. He had written to the Russian actor, theatre director, and teacher **Konstantin Stanislavsky** as early as 1916, sure that there was much in common between his ideas for the Vieux-Colombier and Stanislavsky's work at the Moscow Art Theatre.

Konstantin Stanislavsky (1863 1938) is probably one of the most influential teachers and directors in the history of Western theatre. In 1898 he co-founded, with Vladimir Nemirovich-Danchenko (1858–1943), the Moscow Art Theatre. He revolutionised the actor's craft, building a process through which the actor could repeatedly achieve a high level of psychological realism. He directed the first productions of most of Anton Chekhov's plays. Though stripped of his wealth after the Russian Revolution, he continued to teach, direct and act until his death. His influence owes much to the success of his books, available in English as *An Actor Prepares, Building a Character*, and *Creating a Character*. Recent studies (e.g. Merlin 2003) have highlighted the importance of his later work on Physical Actions and Active Analysis, ideas which share with Copeau's work an emphasis on improvisation and physical engagement with text and character.

Stanislavsky replied to Copeau, excited by the possibility of an international studio which might bring together leading artists from around the world. Copeau was equally enthused, but by the time he attempted to contact Stanislavsky again the February revolution had occurred and Stanislavsky's private fortune and his family's business had vanished. However the friendship which they had established was to endure the distance and difficulties of the next five years, and on the 29 November 1922 Stanislavsky and the Moscow Art Theatre travelled from Berlin to Paris as part of an extensive tour. Copeau was at the Gare du Nord railway station to welcome Stanislavsky, and two days later they met to discuss further the creation of an international centre of theatre art. Copeau and Stanislavsky kept in close contact during the Moscow Art Theatre's visit to Paris and on 21 December a midnight reception was held for Stanislavsky at the Vieux-Colombier. Copeau gave a dinner at a nearby restaurant, also attended by Harley Granville Barker, and then, a few days later, Stanislavsky and his company set sail for New York.

Copeau and his company had the opportunity to watch Stanislavsky's productions of *Fiodor*, *The Lower Depths*, *The Brothers Karamazov*, and *The Cherry Orchard*, and they were very much impressed by what they saw. The opening production of *Fiodor* was nearly a disaster when the sets and costumes did not arrive until the very last minute, however Copeau and his company may have appreciated the subsequent simplicity – all the most elaborate effects were abandoned and the performance took place with the theatre lighting at full throughout. Although they did not know the detail of Stanislavsky's System until much later, when the key texts were translated and published, the Vieux-Colombier company were, in the words of Michel Saint-Denis, 'converted' (Saint-Denis 1967: 111). What Copeau learnt from Stanislavsky was threefold: 'the importance of sincerity and truth, that action must be linked to a psychological state, [and] that movement should originate from need' (Felner 1985: 39). Copeau recognised Stanislavsky as 'the master of us all' (Copeau in Felner 1985: 39), and Stanislavsky's Moscow Studio provided an important model for the future development of the École du Vieux-Colombier.

THE RETREAT TO BURGUNDY – LES COPIAUS (1924–1929)

Stanislavsky's visit to Paris seems to have renewed Copeau's determination to recommit to his original vision for a new kind of theatre. The Vieux-Colombier continued successfully for another year after Stanislavsky's visit, but in 1924 Copeau made the unexpected announcement that he intended to close both School and Theatre. This radical and impulsive decision, taken at a point when his own reputation and that of the Vieux-Colombier was at its height, seemed to many to be a retrograde and capricious step. But for Copeau, the subsequent retreat to the countryside with a small group of young followers represented his final chance to achieve the theatre of which he dreamed. He recognised the enormous risk that he was taking: 'I have left everything. I am playing the last chance of my life' (Copeau in Kusler 1979: 50), but his determination was unshakeable. Copeau 'bequeathed' his Paris company and repertoire to Jouvet before his departure. His influence, through

Jouvet's work and the work of the other members of the **Cartel des Quatres**, would dominate the development of theatre in Paris between the Wars. But this was a world on which Copeau was once more turning his back, setting out to renew his search for a simple, pure and popular theatre – even if it meant starting again almost from scratch.

> The **Cartel des Quatres** was an informal alliance, begun in 1927, between four influential theatres and their directors: Louis Jouvet, Charles Dullin, Gaston Baty, and Georges and Ludmilla Pitoëff. They all committed to a policy of respect for the text, simple staging and a serious approach to the poetic function of drama. It did much both to foster the growth of serious drama production between the Wars, and to protect Copeau's legacy and influence.

In re-locating that autumn to the remote rural village of Pernand-Vergelesses in Burgundy, Copeau was not only committing himself (and the thirty four students, writers, artists and actors who chose to follow him) to the cause of regional theatre, but also in many respects turning his back on Parisian and European modernity in search of a more regenerative vision of theatre (Ward 1996: 173). Disillusioned and disheartened by the failure of his autobiographical play *La Maison natale* (1923) to find favour with the Paris critics, he must also have been facing a crisis of direction. To complicate matters, he was leaving the capital at a time of increasing financial difficulties across Europe, and a time of high taxation for the theatres in France – another possible motive for his decision to close the Vieux-Colombier (Carter 1925: 161). However his intention was not simply to relocate his existing work, but rather to explore a new kind of theatre: a theatre involved in and evolving from the working life of the community in which it was based, producing work relevant to the conditions of life within that community; a theatre which was pure, simple and rigorously focussed on the actor's skills.

Such a retreat attempted also to remove the company from the commercial pressures of the theatre world in Paris. Copeau had spent his early adulthood running a small family factory, and although this had given him a genuine appreciation of the value of craft and honest labour, he must have had no particular desire to find himself permanently tied to the tiller of a theatrical equivalent. At the Vieux-Colombier, the need

for the continuous production of successful performances had increasingly tended to dominate over the activity of the School. Pressure had
grown for a move to larger premises, for the acceptance of subsidy, but
Copeau was reluctant to compromise his vision because of financial
constraints. He must have hoped that the retreat to Burgundy would
allow the balance to shift back in favour of experiment and exploration.
His clear interest in the work with the apprentice group (based largely
on the group of children who had started at the School in 1920) had,
towards the end, created jealousies and divisions within the company
and the School, and the decision to make the break must in part have
meant that he could now draw a line under some of those fractures and
schisms.

In November 1924 Copeau gathered together the small company
(which included his own daughter Marie-Hélène, and the young
Etienne Decroux) in order to announce his aims for his new project.
The emphasis within this enterprise was to be on the moral responsibility of the actor, the importance of personal discipline, respect for fellow
artists, the value of individuality, sincerity, intelligence and good
humour. The organisation of the company in Pernand-Vergelesses was
in many ways a continuation of the regime Copeau had established for
the final year students of the school in Paris. They continued to help with
cleaning, kept a log of their activities and held meetings to discuss their
work (Kusler 1979: 36). The cohesion of the group was strengthened by
the interlocking family units of which it was now composed.

Etienne Decroux (1898–1991) enrolled as a student at the Vieux-
Colombier School in 1923. He followed Copeau to Burgundy, but left after
five months as a result of the company's initial problems. He then worked
with Baty and Jouvet, and later joined Dullin at the Théâtre de l'Atelier as
an actor and mime teacher, where he worked for eight years. In 1931 he
met with the young actor Jean-Louis Barrault, and together they began
working on what was to become the basis of Decroux's concept of
corporeal mime. Decroux performed in mime performances, plays, and
films (including the famous film *Les Enfants du Paradis*), but perhaps his
greatest legacy is as a teacher – alongside the international mime artist
Marcel Marceau (whom he taught) and Jacques Lecoq, Decroux is one of
the central figures in the history of modern mime.

For some of Copeau's literary friends, including the writer André Gide, the retreat to the countryside represented an act of misguided romanticism. For Gide, the sanctity and purity of which Copeau dreamed were a seductive illusion. Gide's criticisms were effectively countered by later commentators (e.g. Bentley 1950: 48–51), who recognised that the important quality of such an experiment was not the end result so much as the process itself. Nonetheless, the retreat to Burgundy was a venture balanced for its success on a knife's edge. Copeau was tired and unwell after years of managing the Vieux-Colombier – his commitment and dedication would not let him slacken, and as with so many of his ventures he found it hard to delegate responsibility. Furthermore, money was short – the Vieux-Colombier had drained a lot of Copeau's personal resources, and the company finances were complicated and confusing. Although Copeau had made thorough preparations for the setting up of the Vieux-Colombier, this new move had been relatively sudden and impulsive and consequently seemed more reckless to his concerned friends. Copeau felt a deep sense of responsibility for his young company, and this transposed itself into a rigorous insistence on self-discipline, re-inforced by various sets of rules and regulations. Copeau's Catholic beliefs led him to insist on an almost monastic devotion to communal self-sufficiency; in those early months living conditions were hard and money was scarce, illness was also rife. The company was forced to throw together two performance pieces, which they presented in Lille as part of an unsuccessful attempt to raise money. By late February, it was clear that the project, as initially conceived by Copeau, could not continue; he had no option but to disband the group.

What Copeau appears not to have expected was the internal momentum which had built up of its own accord amongst his young company. The basic conditions, the return to nature, and the strong sense of community that the retreat had provided, had fostered an instinctive interest in ritual and festivity and in the exploration of dramatic responses to the rhythms and celebrations of the countryside. The strict rules had helped to cultivate a disciplined work-ethic, but had also engendered a rich counter-seam of playfulness, irreverence and spontaneous celebration. A small number of the original group decided to stay on in Pernand-Vergelesses and continue the work, including: Suzanne Bing, **Michel Saint-Denis** and Leon Chancerel (1886–1965).

Michel Saint-Denis (1897–1971) was Copeau's nephew. He became a student at the Vieux-Colombier School and followed Copeau to Burgundy in 1924 to become a key member of Les Copiaus. When the troupe was disbanded Saint-Denis founded the Compagnie des Quinze with his former colleagues and the young company achieved considerable success. He settled in London in the early 1930s and alongside his achievements as a director he also co-founded the influential Old Vic Theatre School. He had a profound influence on the development of actor training in Europe and North America and was one of the original artistic directorate of the Royal Shakespeare Company.

Within a few months, Copeau, assisted by Saint-Denis, had drawn together a new smaller group from the few followers who had stayed on in Burgundy. The company's log-book notes that the local people, punning on Copeau's name, had started to call the group 'Les Copiaus' (or the Little Copeaus). The company now adopted this title, a name which reflected the strong connections with Copeau's vision and yet also suggested lightness, youth and humour. Copeau continued to participate as a writer and an actor, though large portions of his time were also taken up with raising funds through lecture tours and personal appearances. Certainly Copeau's continued presence (however distant at times) meant that he maintained a clear control over the general direction of the work. This arrangement was not without its difficulties and its tensions. For some of Les Copiaus, *le patron*'s control of the group sometimes felt oppressive. Just as Dullin and Jouvet had eventually needed to become independent of the Vieux-Colombier, so too the members of Les Copiaus, already straining at the leash, increasingly sought to explore their own creative instincts. Copeau had always been gifted at developing the talents and creativity of others, and Les Copiaus are a significant success in this respect. The price of his success, however, was that despite being on the verge of achieving his prophetic vision of a small troupe of actor/artists who would tour a repertoire of classic and devised performances to the people, Copeau seems to have struggled to find a new role for himself within this democratic and youthful project.

Les Copiaus' early performances were collages of rural life, which, although initially thrown together in haste, showed an increasing confidence in the new skills and artistic processes which they were acquiring and developing. The performances would typically contain a prologue, short scenes and one-act plays, and entertainments including songs and dances. Characters and scenarios were created and developed through observation, mask-work and improvisation, and then later worked into the performances. The working day for the company and the young students revolved around a programme of gymnastics and mime exercises, voice exercises and general theatre classes in the mornings, followed by improvisation, games, rehearsal, devising and group work in the afternoons. Sessions were also organised to work on mask-making, singing, music and design. The days were long, the work demanding, with each member also taking on general company tasks and responsibilities. All of these features contributed to the company's sense of identity, coherence and purpose, foreseeing the kind of communal practices that would later form the basis of the work of experimental practitioners such as the Polish director Jerzy Grotowski (1933–1999) and the director of the Odin Teatret, Eugenio Barba (1936–).

Protracted and increasingly frequent absences from Pernand-Verglesses, meant that Copeau became progressively more distanced from Les Copiaus and their work. The absences were necessary; despite their relative self-sufficiency the young group still relied upon the income from Copeau's many lectures, readings and other professional activities for their financial survival. In the interim, the company continued to experiment and improvise around their own ideas; the training also continued, led by the older members of the company. As indicated above, such separations between the 'master' and his students eventually created tensions within the community. The younger students found themselves having to adapt to the increasing need to perform rather than train. Their loyalties must also have felt stretched between Copeau and the senior company members who wanted to develop the company's work along their own lines of interest. Suzanne Bing kept a faithful record of the group's work (Gontard 1974), but she clearly felt her position was somewhat compromised by her relationship with Copeau and, possibly as a result, tended to put a generally positive gloss on his absences and the relationship between the group and its *patron*.

Things came to a head in March 1928, when the company premiered a new show, *La Danse de la Ville et des Champs (The Dance of the Town and the Fields)*, which had been devised and rehearsed with very little input from Copeau himself. The first performance took place in front of a full house including old friends, former colleagues and Copeau. For many watching, the performance was a triumph of collaborative creation, an accomplished example of ensemble acting which demonstrated the power and effectiveness of choral movement, physical acting and mask-work (see Rudlin 1986: 109–10 for a full description). The next day the company assembled to hear Copeau's critique of the piece: it was devastating. Expecting notes for improvement, the troupe listened in a state of shock and dismay as Copeau derided their efforts and their work. The actor Jean Villard-Gilles, several years later, still recalled the bitter disappoint of this moment: 'All our efforts, all our passions, all our joy – there was nothing left. Nothing found favour in his eyes' (Villard-Gilles in Rudlin 1986: 110).

There are several possible reasons for Copeau's destructive response to his students' work: possibly he had sought to bring the young troupe, elated by their success, back to earth; perhaps he found it difficult to accept the achievements of the Copiaus without his guiding presence; he might have found the relaxed and easy-going atmosphere that tended to permeate the group in his absence problematic for his natural asceticism; it is even possible that his increasingly strong religious sense found the work ultimately too secular. Whatever the reason, Copeau's crushing dismissal marked a watershed moment in his relationship with Les Copiaus. The company continued for one more year, adding new productions to their repertoire and even devising new collaborative performances (once again without Copeau's participation), but finally dispersed for good in 1929. The core of Les Copiaus was to continue, reforming as the Compagnie des Quinze, under the leadership of Michel Saint-Denis. Although the ways had parted, both Copeau and his former colleagues retained a very warm and real affection for each other – Copeau continued to support his former students' work, and they never forgot the legacies he had left them: of rigour, commitment, passion and creativity. The explorations the group had undertaken had proved that a new commedia was indeed possible; they had brought back to life traditions of masked improvisation and popular theatre which were timely and which offered an invigorating new energy to the theatre. Ironically it was perhaps the very rigour, passion and energy which had made the experiment possible which had in the end brought about its eventual demise. The Vieux-Colombier experiment, which had started at one end of the decade and transformed itself through various stages including the retreat to Burgundy and the work of the Copiaus, had, it seems, reached its natural conclusion. Copeau's project to rejuvenate the theatre had finally reached the fulfilment of its first phase; over the next three decades his former pupils continued the work they had begun together – establishing important regional and national theatre initiatives and passing on the skills and techniques they had acquired under Copeau.

POPULAR THEATRE, THE COMÉDIE-FRANÇAISE, AND SACRED DRAMA (1929–1949)

Once again Copeau's personal theatrical mission was drifting into disarray. In a manner reminiscent of his departure from the Vieux-Colombier, the end of the Burgundy experiment came quite quickly and unexpectedly. At the same time his inner life was going through a period of profound change as he continued to come to terms with the personal and artistic implications of his conversion to Catholicism. For two years he now retreated from practical theatre work as he wrestled internally with his creative impulses and his beliefs, unsure in which direction he should travel next. Eric Bentley (1950: 50) suggests that the tensions between Copeau's Catholicism and his commitment to the rediscovery of dramatic expression were profound and antithetical, leading Copeau eventually to compromise the rigour of his dramatic explorations. Certainly, throughout his life in the theatre, Copeau struggled between public exhibition and celebration, and personal seclusion and self-denial. Inevitably his choice of direction at this point in his life was shaped by the reality that he now lacked a troupe of his own, though he toyed occasionally with the possibility of re-grouping the Vieux-Colombier company (Kurtz 1999: 132). He was by now an international theatrical figurehead, and continued to lecture and give readings both in France and abroad; but he relied upon invitations to direct. His first opportunity was an offer to mount a mystery play, *Santa Ulvina*, at Florence in 1933. The production enabled Copeau make use of a medieval site, the cloisters of Santa Croce, and to explore the potential the site offered for experiment with the position of the audience, the use of the *tréteau*, and the movement of actors across broad open spaces. However, as John Rudlin points out, Copeau's interest at this time was actually less to do with these aspects than with 'his new quest for theatre-as-communion' and 'the actual popularity of theatre' (Rudlin 1986: 116). The strength of Copeau's religious convictions meant that he now believed that any new popular theatre must also be a religious theatre, or at least, as John

Rudlin suggests, a theatre that has a role in revealing and confirming social morality. For Copeau, the idea of a 'popular' theatre was strongly linked with his faith in the social value of the great theatres of the past – of Ancient Greek drama and the European medieval mystery plays – theatres which offered models for simple but profound dramatic expression. Through his talks and his writing, in particular his essay 'Le Théâtre Populaire' (Copeau 1941), he advocated for a decentralised structure for theatre in France, for a theatre that could function not only to rebuild a sense of French cultural pride and identity at a time of German Occupation but also to respect and respond to the diversity of French culture as represented in the regions outside Paris. This was to be one of his most important and lasting legacies, and it is examined in more detail in the Chapter 2.

Copeau's return to Catholicism was the result of several complex factors and much personal soul-searching. Certainly on a wider social and cultural scale we can understand his personal decision as a subconscious response to the increasing spiritual unease that was pervading Europe during the 1930s. There was a common perception in some quarters that society was entering a period of moral danger caused by the pressures of modern urban life, increasing secularisation and threats to national culture. Copeau's work in Florence on two grand-scale religious dramas was clearly part of a search for a new unifying role for theatre. Mass performances, pageants and rallies were popular throughout Europe at this time, though put to very different ends according to national political agendas (i.e. the Nazi mass movement choirs for the 1936 Olympics). The complex issues of nationalism and the expression of national and popular concerns through art were of course to be become pressing concerns with the outbreak of war in 1939.

In 1940, at a time of crisis for the French nation, Copeau was offered the directorship of the Comédie-Française. He had initially been approached about running the theatre in the mid-1930s, but having made his conditions clear he found that the Government fought shy of the kind of changes he proposed, and his appointment was shelved. By 1940 much had changed: France had surrendered to Germany, Paris was occupied, and French theatre needed strong leadership if it was to maintain a valuable cultural role in this difficult environment. This was not a post that he would naturally have sought, and the likelihood is that he thought he might be able to be an agent of long overdue change and renewal. He was only partially successful and resigned several months later, having fallen out with the German authorities and the **Vichy Government**, who demanded that he put pressure on his son Pascal to quit the Resistance (Kurtz 1999: 145). This cannot have been an easy decision for him, and he left Paris again for Pernand in order to escape the 'vanity and *cabotinage*' (Copeau in Rudlin 1986: 118), and to live a relatively quiet life based once more in his beloved Burgundy. News of Michel Saint-Denis' successes in London must have given him cause for great pride, and perhaps encouraged him to continue to direct. Copeau's final major production was a further re-working of the 'mystery play' form, *Le Miracle du Pain Doré (The Miracle of the Golden Bread)*, in 1943. The performance took place in the cloisters of the Hospices de Beaune, and drew extensively on his experiences in Florence, on his previous work on the Greek chorus and the Japanese Nōh Theatre, and on his understanding of Appia's ideas of the relationship between theatre and music (Rudlin 1986: 120).

The **Vichy Government** was established after the Franco-German armistice in June 1940. The agreement allowed Germany control of north and western France, whilst the Vichy Government, lead by Marshall Pétain, retained control of the south (it was based in the city of Vichy) and the French colonial empire. Pétain assumed personal control of the government, effectively dismissing the Senate and the Assembly. To this extent his values of patriotism, family, religion and hard work became the dominant values which he sought to promote within the 'new' France. In 1942 his regime assisted in the deportation of French Jews to the concentration camps.

Despite the exercises in popular religious drama, Copeau seems by the 1940s to have lost the driving passion for his work which marked his earlier years. In part his declining health was to blame, he suffered from thickening of the arteries (atherosclerosis) for a large portion of his later life. He was, as a result, no longer able to take on the sheer volume of work that he had managed in his former days. There are suggestions (Added 1996) that Copeau's writings at this time can be seen as in some senses favourable towards Pétain's right-wing ideology. Such a view represents a misunderstanding of Copeau's passionate pride in his national culture and of his commitment to a theatre which speaks to the common people as well as to the theatrical *cognoscenti*. His writings on popular theatre, his period at the helm of the Comédie-Française, and his epic productions of religious plays are in this sense the activities of a man searching for that which could heal, unite and give purpose to a country riven and humiliated by defeat and occupation. Though his work as a director was minimal after the War, his desire for recognition as a writer did not leave him, and he continued to write plays and to publish articles about his experiences and ideas, up until his death on 20 October 1949 at the Hospice in Beaune – the very place where a few years earlier he had staged his last production.

LE PATRON

The psychological forces that contributed to Copeau's charisma and energy were also the source of some of his inner struggles and personal disappointments. His life was driven by contradictory impulses that must have created powerful tensions for him. Despite a strong moral and religious sensibility, he had several affairs outside his marriage – one of which resulted in a child; it is possible that the pressure of reconciling his sexual energies with the guilt he must have felt as a result of his strong Catholic beliefs may have intensified his zeal for purity, discipline and rigour in his theatre work. Copeau was a man of great energy and conviction, a charismatic figure able to draw others to him and to enthuse them with his own vision; but, although others held him in deep affection, it is difficult to tell how much at peace he was with himself. His intense passion for theatre sometimes meant that he trod a lonely path – he was not a man who found compromise easy, and he demanded the best from himself and from those he worked with. Copeau liked to take on everything himself – he knew every aspect of the making of theatre from personal experience, and he encouraged his students and fellow actors to do the same. If there is one criticism of his dedication and enthusiasm it might perhaps be that it left him too demanding of himself to become a great actor or a great playwright (an ambition he had cherished from childhood). Though he achieved success in both these areas, his real talent lay in directing and teaching, in encouraging, shaping and developing the creative abilities of others. In this he was supremely gifted, and it is here that his influence on the future development of theatre practice and cultural policy was most profound. The next chapter will examine in more detail the significance of his innovations in these areas.

2

COPEAU'S KEY
WRITINGS AND IDEAS

The written word revolutionised the dissemination of ideas and the documentation of practice within early twentieth century theatre. This was the age of the manifesto, the polemical essay, the teaching manual and the call to action. The cultural struggles of the early part of the century, as modernist art sought to overcome the dominance of tradition and the academy, demanded that innovation prepared its own defence; this meant setting out clearly the principles on which new cultural practices were founded. Initially there were few models on which to base such writings – the professional secrets of the actor were jealously guarded, and their social status was such that few writers would consider acting and actors worthy of anything but occasional interest. The nineteenth century interest in scientific analysis spawned several attempts at cataloguing approaches to voice production, posture, gesture and oratory as the profession attempted to claw its way up the ladder of social respectability. For the most part, however, it was a question of drawing on existing models for inspiration. Stanislavsky structured his first book, *My Life in Art* (1924), as an autobiography, a well-established conventional style which his later texts continued to exploit, albeit in a fictionalised format. In contrast, Copeau, before he became an actor and director, was an accomplished writer, critic and essayist who published a large number of articles, reviews, pamphlets and letters on the subject of theatre. It was therefore understandable that the writing style which came naturally to him was neither that of the autobiography nor that of the training manual, but instead that of the essay, the call to action, and the manifesto for change. As a result, his writing is distinctively succinct and purposeful; it is personal without being autobiographical, passionate without being didactic. What it lacks in detail it makes up for in eloquence, erudition and persuasiveness. Copeau never claimed to have a 'system' in the formal sense claimed by Stanislavsky; indeed, Michel Saint-Denis was clear that Copeau, 'never worked from or towards a system' (Saint-Denis 1960: 92). Copeau, late in his life, described himself as 'a friendly adviser who cannot pretend to give advice except from his personal experience' (Copeau 1974: 108–9, author's translation). What his notes and writings convey instead is an overall pedagogical design and a set of principles for the rejuvenation of the theatre rather than a detailed training schedule, and our expectations must be tailored accordingly. Copeau saw no need to record his working methods in detail. On the one hand they were subject to frequent change, experiment and revision; on the other hand, to do so smacked a little too much of a fixed 'system', something that Copeau was determined to avoid. He wrote lists of exercises in note form, recorded the sequence of his work, outlined tasks that needed addressing, reminded himself of key themes to his work, but nowhere does he describe a sustained sequence of exercises or rehearsal methods in any detail. In our contemporary information-hungry culture such reticence may well seem a little perverse or secretive, but for Copeau and his students there was simply no purpose to such a record – their work would speak for them, and for the quality of their processes and practices, and others would learn through the same process of personal transmission.

So busy was Copeau with the practice of his art that it was not until towards the end of his life that he began the difficult task of collecting and editing his extensive collection of writings. In order to create a more structured and permanent record of his work and his ideas, he recorded and published memories of his earlier experiences in *Souvenirs du Vieux-Colombier* (1931). At the same time he also began to collect his notes, articles, letters and papers as part of a project to publish a fuller account of his ideas. His failing health meant that he was unable to complete this task before his death; nonetheless, the project has been continued by his family, his former collaborators, and his friends and admirers. Their efforts have resulted in the posthumous publication (to date) of six volumes of his writings, under the collective title of *Les Registres*.

Broadly, these volumes focus on: his calls for change and rejuvenation within the theatre; his writings on Molière; his work before, during and after his tour to America; and, his experiments in actor training. The only substantial selection of these (and other) texts available in English is *Copeau: Texts on Theatre* (1990), translated and edited by John Rudlin and Norman Paul, which is currently out of print. This chapter will examine several key themes from Copeau's writings, and assess the extent to which they represent a coherent theory for theatrical creation and performance. The aim throughout is to create a clear picture of the theatre towards which Copeau was striving and to better understand how he proposed to get there.

There are three main themes which inform the majority of Copeau's work and writings:

1   the rejuvenation of the theatre;
2   the education of the creative actor; and
3   the role of popular and sacred theatre in a modern society.

These themes reflect many of the key developments taking place in European theatre during this period, and indicate Copeau's importance in the history of twentieth-century theatre practice. They will form the central structure for this chapter, helping us to understand Copeau's ideas and practices within an overall framework and within the intellectual context from which they grew.

THE REJUVENATION OF THE THEATRE

> The renewal of the theatre which has been dreamed of for generations, and which ours is constantly calling for, seems to me to be essentially a renewal of man in the theatre.
>
> (Copeau 1974: 243)

The driving force at the heart of all of Copeau's work was a profound desire to rejuvenate French theatre from what he saw as its tired, over-commercialised, and moribund state at the end of the nineteenth century, and to re-centre it on the central triumvirate of the poet-playwright, the creative actor and the director. In actuality, Parisian theatre during the mid-nineteenth century was, for all its artistic limitations, a thriving and successful industry. This economic success was in no small part due to a willingness to cater directly to the tastes and inter-ests of the urban masses; the result was a theatrical diet that was mainly composed of melodrama and sentimental entertainment. The end of the century was, however, to bring increased economic prosperity and a rapid expansion of industrial production, all of which contributed to a growth in the middle class population and their spending power, and to a gradual subsequent change in the social composition of Parisian theatre-goers. The consequent mild 'gentrification' of theatre audiences also prompted actors and playwrights to aspire towards a more elevated social status, encouraging those who might otherwise have rejected a career in the theatre as too far beneath them to think again. These twin social forces had the effect of driving Parisian theatre in two opposite directions. On the one hand, the theatre became an arena for splendour and pleasure – fashionable society delighted in being seen at plays, actresses were courted by gentlemen fascinated and titillated by the glamour of the theatre, extravagant circus entertainments combining the skilful, the dangerous, the grotesque and the exotic caught the popular fancy. One the other hand, a new generation of theatre-goers, directors, playwrights and actors harboured desires for a 'serious' theatre, capable of engaging with the important issues of the time and of critiquing the complacencies and excesses of the *belle époque*. This new generation, further encouraged by the relaxation of the French laws on theatre censorship around the turn of the century, set their sights on creating a theatre which might, in their view, more truthfully catch the spirit of the times in all its beauty and its squalor and break the mould of conventional nineteenth century drama. Two of the most important figures from this period, both of whom were early influences on Copeau, were André Antoine (1856–1943), director the Théâtre Libre, and Aurélian Lugné-Poë (1869–1940), director of the Théâtre de l'Oeuvre. As early as 1887, Antoine had introduced the idea that acting could represent everyday life faithfully and without artifice. Lugné-Poë, who had performed in Antoine's company, preferred to explore the power of Symbolist drama. His productions emphasised the suggestive and the spiritual, as, for instance, in the Théâtre de l'Oeuvre production of *Pelléas and Mélisande* (1893) by the Belgian symbolist playwright Maurice Maeterlinck (1862–1949); and, like Antoine, he also knew the value of training a disciplined company of actors. The pioneering work of Antoine and Lugné-Poë represented an important first turn of the tide against the melodramatic conventions of the nineteenth century.

The success of the Théâtre Libre and the Théâtre de l'Oeuvre was also economically significant, public subsidy for avant garde theatre was virtually non-existent and consequently the risks involved in theatrical experimentation were substantial. The opportunity to develop new and innovative theatre techniques was effectively unavailable to those without independent financial means. Lacking subsidy or patronage, theatre companies were forced to balance their books through an incessant cycle of performances and tours; inevitably this put severe pressure on rehearsal time or experiment and training. Though Antoine and Lugné-Poë's achievements were not as complete and wide-ranging as Copeau's, their example provided invaluable proof that innovation could be achieved within what was still in effect a commercial industry.

Copeau can have been in no doubt about the enormous challenges involved in rejuvenating French theatre. In his article 'L'École du Vieux-Colombier', he remembers Craig's response to an invitation to become technical director of the Théâtre des Arts: 'that the theatre would first have to be closed to the public for ten or fifteen years in order to allow him to begin his work from the beginning' (Copeau 1990: 27). For Copeau, Craig's response, if impractical, was still logical and represented an honest assessment of the conditions required for genuine and sustainable dramatic renewal. What point was a renewal, he realised, without a deeply informed sense of purpose and without the foundation stones of a thorough and tested methodology.

ART AND COLLABORATION

The programme for the 1917–1918 New York season, announced that the guiding principles of the Vieux-Colombier company's work were: 'modesty, sincerity in arduous research, continuous novelty, absolute refusal of compromise towards commercialism or *cabotinage*' ('French Theatre du Vieux-Colombier': 3). It may be difficult for a twenty-first century reader to recognise the impact of this kind of declaration; Copeau was proposing nothing short of a small revolution – a new concept of 'professionalism' and 'artistry' for the actor. In place of the *cabotin*'s use of easy tricks and pursuit of audience adulation, Copeau was seeking to establish a kind of *confrérie*, or monastic fellowship, of actors dedicated to the refinement of their art, to its continuous renewal and to its artistic and moral integrity. It is from this aim to reinvent the notion of the professional actor that so much else of Copeau's vision flows.

Copeau built his plans to rejuvenate the theatre on two important assumptions – that theatre is an art-form, and that theatre is a collective and collaborative activity. He was passionately committed to the idea of theatre as an art in its own right. For him theatre was a lifetime's vocation, a calling of an almost religious nature. The company tour to America in 1917 convinced him that achievement of his aims lay not in novelty nor in celebrity nor in commercial success, but in a steady and patient discovery of the possibilities open to the artist:

> If the notion of rapid and brutal success can be fruitful in the industrial or commercial world, it is absolutely disastrous from the point of view of art.
>
> (Copeau in Kurtz 1999: 58)

If Copeau's language indicates a suspicion of the 'brutal' nature of industry and commerce (of which he had some first-hand experience), it should not be mistaken as an indication of any strong political affiliation. Like Stanislavsky, Copeau lived through profoundly political times without ever fully engaging with the possible implications for his own theories and practice. Unlike other contemporaries, such as the German socialist playwright and director Bertolt Brecht (1898–1956), Copeau's driving imperatives were predominantly aesthetic rather than political. Copeau seems instead to have had an instinctive preference for a theatre built on an organic creative process developed through patient discovery, turning his back on the modernist theatre of science, technology and mechanisation. Throughout his career he was constantly responding to the changes and challenges which modern life provided, but the pattern of his responses was to retreat from the urban environment to the countryside (e.g. Le Limon and Pernand-Vergelesses) and return to what he understood as the essential elements of the actor's art. This 'return to nature' models the departure of many late nineteenth and early twentieth century European painters for the rural environment, and the establishment of artists' colonies (such as the community lead by the French Post-Impressionist painter Paul Gaugin (1848–1903) at Pont-Aven, or that led by the painter Théodore Rousseau (1812–1867) at Barbizon). The return to a 'simple life' was clearly intended to mark a corresponding return to simple principles grounded in a close association with nature, as well as a rejection of the more formal conventions laid down by the academies and the conservatoires, the official guardians of nineteenth century taste. It is in these respects that

Copeau's aesthetics acquire part of their limited political dimension; in his rejection of the city as the dominant cultural landscape, and of the conservatoire as the arbiter of taste, Copeau attempted to engage with new notions of the artists' relationship to their cultural heritage, and with the manner in which theatre companies could and should operate.

A MODERN RENAISSANCE: MOLIÈRE AND COPEAU

Copeau's principle inspiration for the rejuvenation of the theatre of his time came not from the example of his immediate predecessors, such as Antoine, but from a profound appreciation and critical re-evaluation of the work and achievements of the great French playwright and actor **Molière**. Any attempt at an understanding of Copeau's aims and artistic principles has to make reference to this supreme theatre artist who, in Copeau's eyes, represented the best example of his aesthetic vision. One whole volume of *Les Registres* is dedicated to Copeau's writings on Molière – reviews of performances, discussions of his work, reflections on his own experiences as an actor in and director of Molière's work; Copeau recognised his debt to Molière as substantial and continuing.

Born Jean-Baptiste Poquelin, **Molière** (1622–1673) is one of the great comic writers of all time. His plays, written for his own company Illustre Théâtre, moved beyond the use of stock comic roles to create rich yet instantly recognisable characters. The plays were much more than simple comedies, offering carefully observed, witty critiques of the follies and vices of his time. His most successful plays include: *Tartuffe*, *Le Misanthrope*, *L'Avare (The Miser)*, and *Le Malade Imaginaire (The Hypochondriac)*.

For Copeau, 'Molière is our perfect model because he is essentially an infallible *metteur en scène*, that is, a man whose imagination takes fire from the possibilities of theatre' (Copeau 1990: 143). In this sense, Molière represented the theatre artist *par excellence*, in whose work we can perceive the finest operation of the qualities and features distinctive to theatre as an art-form. For Copeau, the theatre of Molière represented a vision of theatre as a system of signs which has its own internal coherence, a coherence which is ultimately dependent on its own playful, theatrical logic with its own rules. Copeau had a lifetime fascination with games, and in a very modern sense he understands the relationship of the signifying elements within theatre as a game, which can be played with more or less skill and understanding; and for Copeau, 'Molière teaches us the rules of the game' (ibid.: 142).

Copeau thus reaffirmed his belief in theatre as an art-form through reference to the past, a past where he was convinced it was possible to rediscover 'the ancient laws of the theatre' (ibid.: 112). What Copeau means precisely by these 'ancient laws' is less clear – he certainly does not seem to intend the classical 'three unities' of time, space and character for instance. What he does (re)assert is the importance of the imagination as that which, for both actor and audience, connects the various elements to create a 'poetics' for the theatre:

> What I call theatrical convention is the use of infinite combinations of very limited material signs and means, which give the mind a limitless freedom, thus leaving poetic imagination its full fluidity.
>
> (ibid.: 112)

It is in his re-interpretation of the simple fluid staging of the classical theatre of Ancient Greece and of the playhouse theatres of Shakespeare's time that we can perceive the heart of Copeau's aesthetics – it is through the de-cluttering of the theatrical space that it is possible to approach the fullest expression of theatre as a discrete art-form. By purifying the theatrical event, Copeau aims to achieve a condition, which he sees as intrinsic to its aesthetic integrity, where there is 'an identity of means and expression' (ibid.: 116). He believes that the theatre must be allowed to recreate the world through its own resources, its own symbols and rites if it is to fulfil its own potential: 'It communicates with the real world, borrowing its forms, colours and its accents, but gives it back an image composed only from its own resources' (ibid.: 118). We can see then that Copeau's whole aesthetic was essentially humanist in nature. It was based on his belief in the power of theatre 'to unite people of every rank, every class' (Copeau in Auslander 1997: 16), to renew man in the theatre, through an act of 'communion' created by a return to what he understood as the essence of drama.

'A SINGLE ACT': THEATRE AS A COLLABORATIVE ACTIVITY

In a theatre space that is emptied of all but the essential elements, everything that is left onstage becomes imbued with a deeper significance, and with a wider set of imaginative possibilities. The true art of the theatre, in Copeau's eyes, is achieved when, 'Dramatic innovation and its *mise en scène* are but two aspects of a single act. Thus there is no longer any conflict, nor even any difference in the ideas of the poet, the actor and the director' (Copeau 1990: 116). In order to achieve this vision of theatre, Copeau realised that he needed to bring the actor, the playwright-poet and the director closer together:

> I want the poet, having to express himself through the actor, to be as close to him as possible, as associated and incorporated with him as possible, so that the art of one joins with the other.
>
> (ibid.: 117)

Copeau's innovative conception of theatre required not only a new form of staging and a new actor, but also new playwrights, those who would 'know how to write for the actor' (ibid.: 117). The aim of this particular kind of collaboration was to release more fully the creative imaginations of all those involved. To achieve this Copeau also proposed a small revolution in the rehearsal room. In a short essay, first published in 1930, on the role of the poet in the theatre (Copeau 1974: 169–83, extracts in Copeau 1990: 113–19), Copeau gives us a brief sketch of the conventional rehearsal process of the time. In it he illustrates how the playwright-poet faces numerous pressures, especially from lead actors and actresses, to compromise on the artistic vision of the play. These pressures resulted directly from the socio-economic hierarchies within the theatre industry of the time. Copeau recognised that in order for the playwright-poet to reassert his status within the theatre, he must be able 'to correct the errors he is condemning' (ibid.: 118). The playwright-poet can only do so from a position of knowledge, understanding and authority; such a position must be achieved through new approaches to writing, new rehearsal methods and new approaches to theatre education and training. The frustration for Copeau was that few of the playwrights he worked with seemed able to respond to this challenge (with the possible exception of Charles Vildrac, Jules Romains, and

Georges Duhamel). He believed that by providing the right artistic environment he could somehow invoke the writers of the future. To some extent limited success was inevitable, given that Copeau's aims and ambitions were so remarkably new for his time, and that the only models he had to offer aspiring playwrights were the daunting colossi of Molière and Shakespeare. He was, unfortunately, ahead of his time; it was to take several generations for his dreams to be fully realised. The modern notion of the playwright-in-residence is a direct legacy of Copeau's practice, and whilst a true spirit of collaboration is still far from the norm within many company structures Copeau would certainly have approved of the integrated collaborative approaches of companies such as Joint Stock/Out of Joint and Théâtre de Complicité, where the writer, the director, the designer and the performers come together towards the achievement of Copeau's 'single act'.

The following sections will examine in more detail the implications of Copeau's ideas on collaboration and collective creation for the practice for the performer, the designer and the director.

ALL FOR ONE, AND ONE FOR ALL: THE CHORUS

For Copeau, the art of acting is not simply the art of a talented individual, it is an ensemble art: 'the Chorus is the mother-cell of all dramatic poetry' (Copeau in Paul 1987: 582). We have already seen that Copeau believed that 'there is only one great personality . . . who has the right to dominate the stage: that is the poet; and through him the dramatic work itself' (Copeau 1990: 11), but it is a humble dominance because it cannot be achieved without the cooperation of others. Copeau saw the star-system of the boulevard theatre of his time as deeply detrimental to the moral and aesthetic integrity of the theatre. His preference for a choral approach was not simply based on a rejection of current convention, it also had a philosophical basis. He was influenced by the idea of *unanisme*, a philosophical position proposed by his colleague Jules Romains, which emphasised the social over the individual and the merging of the one into the many. In searching for a working theatrical environment in which such aims could be implemented Copeau identified several models (ibid.: 166). At the heart of each model circulated a specific idea of community:

- the Greek chorus, or *le choeur*, represented a group of performers acting as a coherent dramatic unity within a shared moral, social, political and religious framework;

- the commedia dell'arte troupe or the circus family represented a close-knit band of performers drawing on a rich tradition of improvisation and physicality, and sharing the economic realities of producing and performing their work;

- the monastic brotherhood and the medieval mystery play performers represented a group of people united by religious beliefs and by specific forms of creative self-sufficiency.

Copeau's work, through the early Vieux-Colombier company to the Copiaus troupe, can be seen as a gradual development towards his own synthesis of these models into a working company system suited, in its own specific ways, to the modern cultural environment. The closeness, understanding and loyalty engendered within such models are reflected in the strong personal ties which grew to bind his company members together for so long. The companies acted as a kind of social support system, drawing in children, relatives, friends and supporters. Such camaraderie also enabled the development of a rapport between actors whilst on stage; vital qualities of trust, vulnerability, openness, playfulness and risk-taking are all encouraged within a company that shares such a sense of community and common purpose. Not only were the individual performances of a more consistent standard, but the quality of the whole ensemble performance was also on a different level. Copeau's rigour as a director, and his insistence that the task of all involved was to discover the best theatrical expression of the playwright-poet's 'voice', meant that his actors performed with style, consistency, precision and familiarity.

DESIGN: A MINIMUM OF MEANS

As early as the Vieux-Colombier's productions of *La Nuit des Rois* and *Les Fourberies de Scapin* Louis Jouvet and Copeau were taking responsibility not only for acting and direction, but also for innovations in theatre design and lighting. The result was a set of unified design concepts which aimed to release the actors' creativity and enhance their imaginative engagement with the set, costumes and props. The nakedness of Copeau's stage space left the modern actor exposed as never before, but it also positively enabled the imagination of the poet, the actor and the

director, by removing the artificial props on which they would otherwise have leant. The first re-design of the Vieux-Colombier theatre
space in 1913 had preserved a proscenium arch arrangement over the
stage, and some limited wing space. After the New York tour, Jouvet
and Copeau set about further simplifying the structure of the theatre, by
removing the proscenium arch and stripping back the space to a basic
open arena with simple exit points. This clearly placed the work of the
Vieux-Colombier alongside that of the other experimental theatre
practitioners of the day who sought to reject the formal picture-box
naturalism or stage trickery so strongly associated with conventional
illusionist drama.

At the back of the new space Copeau and Jouvet provided: a simple
arch over an alcove, not unlike the Elizabethan 'tiring house', which
could act as a space for concealment or revelation, or as another
entrance/exit; and, stairs to provide further entrance/exit points on
different levels. The open fixed staging, or *dispositif*, and also the use of
simple levels, was designed to enable choral and choreographed physical
movement, a dynamic use of three-dimensional space, and economic
and theatrically effective use of limited design resources. Even the
smallest alterations to the fixed staging became immediately more elo-
quent and resonant. For *Le Pacquebot Tenacity* the alcove area became the
door and windows to a little café, and the only other additions were a
bar, several tables and some stools. For *Les Fourberies de Scapin* the main
additions were the rostra blocks which formed the *tréteau nu*. The simple
staging both encouraged and emphasised the physical skills of the actors.
The radical clarity and simplicity of all the scenic elements in the theatre
was a cornerstone of Copeau's mission to establish an environment
in which genuine theatrical rejuvenation could take place. Without
doubt he was consciously evoking the great theatres of the past in his
architectural designs, however he managed successfully to avoid slavish
authenticity and create a space which was flexible, dynamic and open to
transformation.

The simplicity of Copeau's designs was completely consistent with
his general ideas on theatre. Any extravagant or heavily symbolic stage
design gave too much importance to aspects which Copeau saw as
essentially tangential to the theatrical event: 'Being in favor of this or
that decorative formula always means being interested in theatre by way
of its side-issues' (Copeau in Guicharnaud 1967: 301). He rejected the
importance of stage machinery for the future of the theatre – 'we intend

Figure 2.1
The *tréteau* on the Vieux-Colombier stage (1920)

to deny the importance of all machinery' (ibid.) – believing instead that the discovery of the new theatre could only come by returning to a 'bare stage'.

THE DIRECTOR AND THE TEXT

For Copeau, the text was at the centre of the theatre event. It was the source material which gave meaning to the actor's creativity; the justification for the elimination of extraneous stage decoration and egotistical acting practice lay in the requirement to focus first and foremost on the needs of the text.

> [T]he Théâtre du Vieux-Colombier tries to put in the first place and in full light the work itself, in its truth, in its exact style; and through the action, the staging and the play of the actors, to release the spirit of the poet from the text of the play. From this arises the absolute simplification, even the suppression of scenery. Due to this is the banishing of stars.
>
> (from 'French Theatre du Vieux-Colombier' programme for the 1917–1918 New York season, Fonds Copeau, Bibliothèque nationale de France, p. 5)

The role of the director was therefore to facilitate the unified and coherent expression of the playwright's vision, bringing into conjunction the various elements of the theatre arts, including acting, design, movement, rhythm, space, diction, energy, vitality and spontaneity. As a director, what Copeau brought to his work that was so important for the theatre practitioners that followed after him was a synthesis of the various elements which make for a vital and vibrant theatre – physically expressive characterisation, simple staging, rhythmic structure and ensemble acting. He applied the modern movement techniques of Jaques-Dalcroze and Hébert to the actor's physical expression; and, he applied Craig and Appia's visions of the plastic actor in three-dimensional space, all to develop his own fluid and expressive *mise en scène*.

Copeau's aim as a director was to encourage the actor to react creatively and spontaneously to the script; to this end, he would encourage the actors to get up on their feet as soon as possible, script in hand, and sketch out the outline of the character in action, whilst he exhorted those who struggled with this kind of freedom from the sidelines, saying, 'Go ahead: do something: do anything' (Kusler 1979: 18). This emphasis on action and on getting the actors to commit to 'living' the text as soon as possible actually pre-figures Stanislavsky's **Method of Physical Action**. Though Copeau and Stanislavsky were arriving at this point at different times and from different directions, both seem to have been drawn towards a shared realisation of the importance of engaging the actor in the part through action and improvisation rather than through discussion.

In the last three years of his life (1935–1938) Stanislavsky changed the sequencing of the rehearsal process in order to place an earlier emphasis on the actor exploring the role through personal active identification using improvisation. The actor was to enter the life of the role through enacting the relevant situations rather than through passive analysis. This became known as the **Method of Physical Action** (see Merlin 2003).

Allowing the actors to explore the world of the script through play, improvisation and action enabled them to become more creatively involved in the production even though Copeau, as the director, would retain overall control, editing and choreographing the material they produced. Through this active rehearsal process the design would also be made to come alive, binding the set, lighting and costume into an overall theatrical vision of the play.

This design of a dramatic action is the *ensemble* of movements, of gestures and of attitudes, the harmony of faces, of voices, of silences. It is the totality of the scenic spectacle, emanating from the one thought which conceives it, rules it and harmonises it. The director creates this secret and invisible bond and has control of the personages – this bond which is a reciprocal sensibility, a mysterious reciprocal relation, without which the drama, even interpreted by excellent actors, loses the greater part of its effect.

(Copeau in Miller 1931: 80–1)

The achievement of this vision for a new ensemble theatre company, central to Copeau's mission to rejuvenate the French theatre, was of course reliant on bringing together artists equipped with appropriate qualities of openness and creativity. From the very beginning Copeau realised that anything less than training a new generation of theatre artists would be a compromise.

THE EDUCATION OF THE CREATIVE ACTOR

Almost every significant theatre practitioner of the early twentieth century has sought to confront the problem of preparing actors for a new theatre. Each recognised that it was only through retraining the actor that theatre could achieve a more complete realisation of its own possibilities. Copeau firmly believed that a renewal of the sort that he desired 'must begin with the human being' (Copeau 1974: 109, author's translation). Copeau's contribution needs to be examined in this light, and in relation to the efforts of others such as Stanislavsky, Meyerhold, Chekhov and Craig to reconfigure the human figure of the actor in relation to the stage event. Copeau was aware of many of the innovations in theatre, dance, movement and education which were taking place throughout Europe in the inter-War years. He knew of the movement teachings of Emile Jaques-Dalcroze (with whom he briefly collaborated) and of Isadora Duncan, of the developments in gymnastic training at the start of the century (in particular the work of Georges Hébert), and of the popular physical techniques of the circus clown.

In formulating his own teaching methodology he sought to synthesise an interest in experiment and innovation with a respect for spirituality and tradition. These contradictory aims created strong tensions within his own acting, directing, teaching and playwriting; tensions which meant that he was to take a more conservative direction than other more radical practitioners, but which also allowed his work to have a more immediate and sustainable influence on the development of professional theatre practice. This section will examine the key principles which inform Copeau's education for the actor. It will examine the ideas on which his pedagogy is based, and explore the relationship between these ideas and the central features of his teaching practice:

- improvisation
- mime
- animal/nature studies
- the development and use of mask work.

Copeau realised that sustainable change was impossible without actors who not only desired the creation of a new theatre, but who also possessed the skills and techniques to make it happen. His pedagogy developed over several phases, drawing together and synthesising various practices and influences. It is possible to trace his journey over sixteen years of almost continuous experiment and exploration: from the first exercises in physical training, rehearsal process and improvisation with his actors at Limon in 1913; through his work with Suzanne Bing and the Vieux-Colombier School (first in 1915, later in New York from 1917 to 1919, and then again from 1920 to 1924); to the final experiments with Les Copiaus in Pernand-Vergelesses from 1924 to 1929. Throughout all of these periods of change and development, at the heart of Copeau's training regime was a profound creative journey for the student. His is a pedagogy based on self-discovery, on a rich social and cultural awareness, and on process before product. He was inspired by Jaques-Dalcroze's belief that: 'It is the pupil who should teach the master, not the reverse. The role of the master is rather to reveal to the pupil what it is that he has learned' (Jaques-Dalcroze in Copeau 1990: 57). Along with Stanislavsky, Craig and Appia, he proposed that the standards against which the training of the actor should be measured ought to be set not in respect of the narrow demands of a moribund and conservative theatre industry, but, in a typically modern sense, against a more profound sense of what it meant to be human and to be operating within the boundaries of a living and vibrant art form.

'THE ORIGINAL CRUCIBLE': TRAINING AND THE CHILD

For Copeau the innocent, imaginative play of the child was a central building block for the new theatre. At the heart of his plans was the intention to start training a new generation of actors from an early age; for Copeau, this meant starting during childhood. He was widely read, and his ideas may have been stimulated by some knowledge of the early training given to children in Asian theatre; however, instead of imposing a rigorous and disciplined regime of traditional techniques on his young pupils, Copeau proposed a training that would release their imaginative energies: 'Encourage children in their play, the creative activity of free and happy children in a new world every hour of their imaginative existence' (Copeau 1990: 9). The inspiration for this approach came in part from a philosophical appreciation of the value of imaginative play, but also in some substantial measure from his own childhood, and from his observation of his young children Pascal, Hedvig (Edi), and Marie-Hélène (Maiène).

I have beside me three children whose unconscious genius amazes me. I have seen them create without effort, forms, colours, objects, costumes and disguises, invent actions, plots, people and characters, in a word transfigure everything that came near them.

(Ibid.)

In children's play Copeau saw both an attractive form of naturalness and the creative use of fantasy. He was drawn towards the unselfconscious absorption of children in simple tasks, and their ability to transform those same tasks imaginatively whilst maintaining a coherence within their games. Copeau shared his experiments in the training of children and his exploration of children's games and play with his assistant Suzanne Bing. Bing had observed new educational practices during the New York tour, where she had led drama sessions at the 'Children's School' run by **Margaret Naumburg** (Rudlin 1996: 18). On her return to Paris, her willingness to explore pedagogical methods, to synthesise various performance techniques, and to devise new teaching techniques made her indispensable to the success of the new School.

Margaret Naumburg (1890–1983) was a progressive educator and a pioneer of modern arts therapy theory and practice. The wife of the writer Waldo Frank (a supporter of Copeau's work), she trained in psycho-analysis before also studying with F. M. Alexander in England and with Maria Montessori in Italy. She believed in the liberating effects of play; in the value of intuitive, non-verbal and creative practice; and, in the ability of artistic expression to reveal and harness deep inner psychological forces.

Copeau's interest in the creative education of children has to be understood in relation to a general European interest in educational reform and the arts. The liberal humanist principles of **Jean-Jacques Rousseau**, and the subsequent educational reforms of **Friedrich Froebel** and **Johann Pestalozzi**, eventually helped to change the education of European children from a harsh and functional indoctrin-ation to a process of discovery and learning through play. As the social status of the performing arts improved during the early years of the last century, it became increasingly acceptable for parents to send their children to schools which provided training in dance and theatre skills. The rapid rise of interest in physical education, dance and movement during the early decades of the twentieth century can be evidenced by the successful establishment of schools by key practitioner/ teachers such as Isadora Duncan, Emile Jaques-Dalcroze, and Rudolf Laban.

Jean-Jacques Rousseau (1712–1778) was, amongst many other things, an unconventional and highly influential thinker. He contributed to educational reforms, proposed the moral superiority of the 'natural' over the 'civilised', and wrote an important defence of civil liberty, *The Social Contract* (1762).

Friedrich Froebel (1782–1852) and **Johann Pestalozzi** (1746–1827) were educational reformists, influenced by Rousseau's writings, who developed the learning environment of the '*kindergarten*' and championed education built on play and the natural engagement of the child's senses. The work of all three has had a profound influence of the development of children's education over the last two centuries.

If theatre and dance were now being rediscovered as art forms, capable of noble and profound expression, then an education in such arts might equally have general educational value for children as well as benefits for their technical development as performers. For Copeau, starting with the child pupil was a way of subverting the pernicious influence of the old vocationalism of the *cabotin*; every effort could be made to ensure that the young charges did not succumb to the corrupting temptations of commercial theatre. What children offered as performers was a particular kind of sincerity, something Copeau called, 'authentic inventiveness' (Copeau 1990: 12) and which he saw as so important that the learning experience was for him two-way: 'We observe the children at play. They teach us. Learn everything from children' (ibid.).

TRAINING THE NATURAL ACTOR

The 'authentic inventiveness' of the child which Copeau's pedagogy sought to encourage in his student actors was a direct challenge to the *cabotinage* of the Parisian boulevard theatre. Copeau saw such vocationalism as encouraging the deformation of an actor's talent. Conventionally, actors at this time were trained and hired directly in relation to their ability to perform very specific roles. Graceful gesture and an appropriately declamatory style were prioritised over spontaneity, vigour and imagination. An ability to play a set role in a conventional style, known as an actor's *emploi*, was all that an actor was expected to aspire to. The training of the Paris Conservatoire represented a primary mechanism through which the dominance of such a system was sustained and nourished. Specific traditional skills and techniques were prioritised through the Conservatoire training regimes, which were constructed around dominant knowledges of the body-as-mechanism. Copeau vowed that within his school, the student actor should, at the earliest stage, be firmly guided away from declamation and artificiality and encouraged instead to generate varied, multiple, fluid and 'natural' means of expression. This new actor was to be trained as a company member, not as a 'star'. Copeau associated the *cabotin* with the 'total mechanisation of the person' and with 'the absolute lack of profound intelligence and true spirituality' (Copeau 1990: 253), such actors could not give themselves to the 'single act', nor allow themselves to be absorbed by the character. Inspired by the playful inventiveness of the child, Copeau proposed to train performers who could engage in an uninhibited manner with their environment, so as to create a vivid and tangible sense of 'naturalness', a condition defined by its organic fluidity, by its lack of self-consciousness or artificiality, and by its rejection of conventional interpretations of theatrical roles.

The paradigms which underpin Copeau's notion of the 'natural' performer are not simple or straightforward and merit further examination. For Copeau that which was 'natural' on stage was so not as the result of idle convention, nor as the result of slavish imitation, but because it was naturally and unselfconsciously theatrical, because it engaged the dramatic imagination of both the actor and the spectator. In order to achieve this new 'naturalism', the actor needed to relearn the simple skills of play, the ability to respond directly and imaginatively to the dramatic circumstances, and to rediscover the expressive power of the body committed to dramatic action. The main cultural paradigms which inform Copeau's vision for the re-education of the actor were: the purity of childhood, and the return to nature:

> The primitive tribesman who throws himself down before the rising sun or accompanies the last rays of the day with a mournful chant, the child who, in sheer bodily delight, jumps and shouts for joy on a spring morning: that is where to find the origin of exultation. Whatever may have been, as one century followed another, the forms that dramatic inspiration and play have assumed, let us not forget that they have a sacred origin deep in the heart of man.
>
> (Copeau 1990: 5)

Copeau here implies the role of theatre in returning society to a 'lost state of grace', which fits well with his strong sense of spirituality. The idealised image of the 'primitive' is tinged with anthropological nostalgia; the writing reveals a wistful admiration for those lives seemingly unfettered by the pressures and frustrations of cosmopolitan life. This fascination with the 'primitive' and ritual roots of human culture is not uncommon to other writers and artists at this time (see Innes 1993). Nor is Copeau alone in his belief in a common (ancient) origin for childhood play, ritual ceremony and dramatic expression, as the writings of others such as the **Cambridge Ritualists** testify.

The **Cambridge Ritualists** was a group of early twentieth-century Oxford and Cambridge scholars, which included Jane Harrison (1850–1928), Gilbert Murray (1866–1957), Francis Cornford (1874–1943), and Arthur Cook (1873–1949). They were together responsible for promoting the study of ancient ritual and its connection to drama (specifically in Ancient Greece), suggesting that both had a common root.

Copeau asserts that:

> The original crucible where we forge the creative power which stays with us all our lives, though often diminished, is to be found in the impregnable silence of the child, his sad reveries, his faculty for furnishing a refuge for his anticipations under a table or in a cupboard.
>
> (Copeau 1990: 6)

He may be revealing some details of his own childhood experiences, but, importantly, he is also revealing assumptions about the task which faces the actor. The role of the performer is, in this context, to 'expend the treasures we accumulated under the protection of our youthful guisings. We reveal one by one all the secrets of our childhood and adolescence' (ibid.). The trainee actor returns to the games of childhood not only in order to develop further their skills in improvisation and imagination, but also to rediscover a form of playing/acting which is more 'authentic', more connected to the organic sources of the actor's creativity, more 'natural'. The 'child/actor' nurtures their innate capacity for imaginative play whilst giving it focus. In this respect,

> The method should follow the natural development of the instinct for play in the child, encouraging this, giving him focal points, procuring for him the means for self-expression according to his taste, imagination and need for entertainment.
>
> (Copeau 1931: 92)

The innocence of the child is of course balanced by curiosity, the desire for knowledge. Copeau sought to channel such curiosity, as he himself had done, into the exploration of theatre itself:

> I wanted to undo and reconstruct the instrument of the theatre, as a child takes apart a toy as a diversion, one might say, from its original purpose, its accepted use, and to force it to become something approaching a higher fancy of the mind.
>
> (Copeau 1990: 8)

But as Rudlin points out (1986: 6), what years of misuse had helped take apart, it would take Copeau a whole lifetime to begin re-assembling. Rediscovering the simple play of the child would mean first removing the accretion of years of bad habits, habits ingrained in the very body of the student actor.

BEGINNING WITH THE 'NATURAL' BODY

From the time of his first retreats to Le Limon with the 1913 Vieux-Colombier company we can see repeated evidence of Copeau's continuing belief in the revitalising powers of nature. His regular retreats to the countryside represent a continuing process of 'de-urbanisation', predicated on a concept of urban life as essentially alien to the individual's holistic development. For Copeau, one important key to achieving his mission lay in developing a troupe of actors 'whose pure souls and minds remained unsullied' (Copeau in Rudlin 2000: 56). The metropolitan environment seemed to Copeau to encourage actors to focus on superficial, career-orientated and mindlessly fashionable concerns rather than the development of their art. The return to a rural environment, envisioned as closer to nature, was, for Copeau, a return to a state of being that was less fettered, less corrupted, less divided from itself. By the time Les Copiaus was finally disbanded, his actors had negotiated a pattern of working and co-existing which brought them closer to the rhythms of the rural communities within which they lived, associating more deeply with the rural French models of work, celebration and cultural identity.

Copeau had a lifelong distrust of anything which smacked of artificiality. In seeking to refine the skills and techniques required of the actor, he wanted the actor to achieve the kind of 'strength and simplicity' which he admired in other craftsmen (Rudlin 1986: 45). This quality was built on an integrity of purpose which began with the body and the physical actions of the artisan. Copeau had eventually rejected Jaques-Dalcroze's Eurhythmics as the physical training system for his students because he felt it encouraged the actor to become too self-conscious in their movement. Instead he had turned to the 'natural' gymnastics of Georges Hébert for the physical training of his actors. Hébert's ideas had developed from his observations of the easy and relaxed physical lives of 'primitive' (or pre-industrial) peoples; his 'natural' movements emphasised efficient, purposeful and economic use of the body, which appealed to Copeau's artistic puritanism. The examples that exist of Copeau's movement and mask improvisation exercises indicate a fascination with the physical lives of the working man or woman, but without the cloying sentimentalism of the melodramas and popular entertainments of the time.

Copeau's emphasis on the physical training of actors was thus an integral part of his mission to rejuvenate the theatre. It was also thoroughly modern in that it was in line with the contemporary public interest in physical culture, movement analysis, expressive gymnastics and modern dance. Yet at the same time, the extent to which attitudes to the body and its physical education had changed rapidly over the early decades of the twentieth century, reflected a deep concern over the ways in which modern life was increasingly alienating people from nature, and from a more 'natural' and organic engagement with their physical life. Copeau, like Hébert, believed that human physiology was being deformed through the influences of fashion and modern industrial/urban life.

> Espousing a noble savage theory (echoing Rousseau), Hébert believed that man in his natural state followed normal muscular development, learning to use his body efficiently to cope successfully with nature's environment.
>
> (Felner 1985: 40)

Urban life had narrowed and reduced man's interaction with the natural world, allowing 'natural' physical aptitudes to atrophy. Hébert's system aimed to counteract such effects through the utilisation of complete, whole body activity in 'natural' tasks.

> Implicit in the acceptance of Hébert's ideas is the acceptance of a new aesthetics, based on an unstylised view of physical beauty, independent of all sense of fashion.
>
> (Ibid.: 41)

The attractions of such a system for Copeau were several. It offered students the opportunity to develop a sense of natural and instinctive physicality. It supported the development of 'playfulness' and took the actors' attention out into the world around them. It provided enhanced physical technique in a manner which complemented Copeau's interest in paring away stylistic accretion towards a simple and direct connection between body, intention and expression. Hébert was himself, for a brief period, one of the teaching staff at the École du Vieux-Colombier. Due to the pressure of other commitments he was eventually replaced by one of his assistants, M. Moyne, and later still the classes were taught by Jean Dorcy and Jean Dasté, two of Copeau's own students. What Hébert helped develop was a flexible and confident athleticism which was to become a hallmark of Copeau's work, and of the later work of many of his ex-students and former colleagues (e.g. the Compagnie des Quinze).

THE PHYSICALLY EXPRESSIVE ACTOR

Copeau was determined to get this element of the training right; for him, as for Meyerhold, physical training and the development of the actor's powers of expression were central to the education of the new actor. Furthermore, he realised that such physical authority was useless unless the actor was equipped with the understanding and sensitivity to make good use of it. To this end, other studies (for example art, philosophy and literature) were included in order to cultivate the student's whole personality, and, for the younger students, voice work and diction were equally informed by play, improvisation, movement and rhythm. As Mira Felner points out, the number of movement training courses at the School reflects Copeau's commitment to the value and importance of the physical training of the actor:

> First we must give him an obedient body. Then one draws out of gymnastics the concept of the interior rhythm, then music, dance and masked mime – the word, to elemental dramatic forms, to conscious play, to scenic invention, to poetry.
>
> (Copeau 1931: 92–3, translated in Felner 1985: 40)

The 1922–1923 Syllabus for the School included several sessions aimed specifically at developing the students' physical skills and powers of expression, for example:

2. *Dramatic Training.* Instructors: Jacques Copeau and Suzanne Bing
   Cultivation of spontaneity and invention in the adolescent. Story-telling, games to sharpen the mind, improvisation, impromptu dialogue, mimicry, mask-work, etc. Stage presentations of the various abilities acquired by the students in the course of their general instruction. . . .
6. *c. Dance.* – Instructor: Mlle Lamballe
   Technical study of the steps and figures of classical dance.
   Dramatic applications.
7. *Physical Culture.* Monitor M. Moyne
   Hygiene and training of the body. Open-air exercises.
   Suppleness. Breathing. Endurance. Stability.
8. *Acrobatics, games of strength and skill.* Instructors: Paul and François Fratellini
   Work in the ring of the Medrano Circus.

(Copeau 1990: 43–4)

This is a list which gives witness to the breadth and depth of physical training and improvisation to which the young students were exposed. The blending of traditional skills with those of the acrobat, the clown, the commedia actor and the story-teller is a remarkable innovation, attractive even now. It is appropriate then to look in closer detail at the ideas and principles underpinning some specific key practices within Copeau's pedagogy: games, animal study, and mime.

GAMES: REDISCOVERING PLAY

For Copeau, games provided a crucial link between the innocent and imaginative play of the child, the art of improvisation, and the act of theatrical creation. Games created a place for the trainee actor where fantasy, poetry and reality could mix and interact in the same way that Copeau had experienced as a child. Games offer a space for the student performer where they can totally commit themselves without inhibition. The experience is unselfconscious and yet, at the same time, developmental – the pedagogy is unforced and the motivation to learn is inherent and not imposed. Games were not just a training device for the development of technical skills, they also prepared the actor for performance, encouraging playfulness, imagination, spontaneity and flexibility. As Frost and Yarrow (1990) point out, games 'socialise' the actor's training; Copeau must have been attracted by the way in which games function to draw student actors into mutual reliance for their personal development.

Copeau was truly innovatory in his use of games within actor training – his work with Suzanne Bing is perhaps the first modern example of games being employed in a professional actor training regime. His work pre-dates that of later teachers such as **Clive Barker** and **Keith Johnstone** by several decades.

Clive Barker (1931–2005) was an actor with Joan Littlewood's Theatre Workshop before becoming a teacher and lecturer. His book, *Theatre Games* (1977), remains one of the key texts on the use of games in actor training and rehearsal process. **Keith Johnstone** (1933–) began as a writer at the Royal Court Theatre in London before becoming a teacher of improvisation. His books *Impro: Improvisation and the Theatre* (1981) and *Impro for Storytellers* (1999) provide a wealth of ideas for the use of improvisation games in performance.

Copeau's own notes succinctly summarise the value and importance of games to his pedagogy, underlining their integral role in the actor's development.

All instruction to be like a big game, where one feels more and more carried
away by the development of one's faculties.

Let it not smack of pedagogy.

Play should remain as free as possible.

The entire experience of the child comes from playing.

He then chooses a game according to his inclination, his personality.

He is sincere and true to himself.

(Copeau 1990: 11)

The emphasis that Copeau gives to freedom reveals his intuitive preference for spontaneity over regulation. Copeau insisted that his students maintained a disciplined approach to their work, but for him games functioned as a stimulus for imaginative play and not as a dramatic form in their own right. The game thus assists the student's general education. It creates imaginative and playful links between the world around them and the world of dramatic invention. At the same time, its immediacy and spontaneity protect the students from false theatricality. It was observation of his own children's games that inspired Copeau and Bing to develop the idea of animal improvisations.

ANIMAL STUDY

Animal improvisations were introduced as part of the movement improvisation training some time after Copeau and Bing's first explorations with Eurhythmics and Montessori techniques during the late 1910s; by the opening of the School in 1920 it was part of the syllabus. Again, this would appear to be the first use of this kind of improvisation exercise in formal actor training, though it has subsequently become a staple exercise for European acting students. The origins of this exercise lie in Copeau and Bing's observation of children's games. The exercise grew and developed in sophistication as they both gained in confidence and experience. The study of animal movement had, by this time, acquired scientific and cultural significance and credibility through the detailed observation and analysis of the movement of animals and people by the French movement theorists **Étienne Marey**, **Georges Demeny**, and **Paul Souriau**, and by the pioneer photographer **Eadweard Muybridge**.

Étienne Marey (1830–1904) developed early devises for the recording of movement. He published a book on his studies of human and animal movement entitled, *La Machine Animale* (1873). **Georges Demeny** (1850–1917) was a disciple of Marey, who further refined the use of photographic techniques in the recording of movement. **Paul Souriau** (1852–1926) brought a more philosophical analysis to the study of animal and human movement. Souriau focused on the delight we take in movement – a theme central to his book, *The Aesthetics of Movement* (1889). **Eadweard Muybridge** (1830–1904) was an Anglo-American pioneer of early motion photography, his rapid series of photographs of a horse galloping (1878) proved for the first time that there was a moment when all the horse's hooves were off the ground.

Copeau sought acting which was sincere and 'authentic', where the voice and movement expressed intention with simple conviction. The relatively simple physicality of animals provided an important paradigm. Their movement was efficient and purposeful, yet evocative of intention and even character. Animal improvisations encouraged the student to engage the whole body, to escape from their habitual self-consciousness, and to use observation and analysis as the way into their 'role'. The impossibility of literal transformation means that the emphasis must change to the rhythm and dynamics of the student's movement, to their concentration and commitment to the task, and to the powers of their imagination. The physical skills developed through Hébertism and the playfulness and imagination developed through games could now begin to develop towards dramatic goals. On another level, animal studies encouraged the student actor to engage in a more profound way with the world around them. By temporarily removing the student from text and words, Copeau and Bing enabled identification to be established at a primal physical level. This universalism, where the student can discover and express the 'essence' of the world through movement, could then become the central building block for the development of a renewed theatre served by actors able to identify and reveal the dramatic essence of the playwright-poet's vision.

SILENT IMPROVISATIONS AND MIMED ACTIVITIES

The work of the craftsman represented for Copeau an important and worthy paradigm for simple and effective natural movement; their gestures and movements 'are sincere, they observe real time and correspond to a useful end toward which they are perfectly appropriate' (Copeau in Kusler 1979: 19). Silent improvisation directed the student's focus onto analysis-through-action, emphasising the importance of experience in the study of physical activity. The enemy of the physical actor was self-consciousness, a failure to commit themselves fully to the action they were required to play; through mimed action the student was required to commit fully to the physical task, there was nowhere else to hide. Mimed action was more than an economic form of *mise-en-scène*, Copeau also believed that movement was involved in the creation of specific states of consciousness. Instead of the actor studying a character's 'inner state of mind', he preferred the actor to allow the movement to generate the character's mental state. By committing to the character's actions, the actor was also committing to the character's state of mind.

The study of everyday work activities generated an appreciation of efficient physical movement, where all the actor's attention is focussed on achieving the intended aim. Early movement analysis had already demonstrated that rhythm was an important feature in efficient movement. Suzanne Bing's experiments with rhythmical movement now informed the development of the silent mime improvisations at the School, allowing students to give their improvisations dynamic energy and a sense of internal structure. Working in silence also avoided the temptation to 'short-cut' the actor's work through an easy recourse to language. The actor had no alternative but to physically inhabit the world of the improvisation, recognising *action* as the pulsing heart of drama. Silence allowed the focus to fall squarely onto the actions of the student – every movement was thus subjected to scrutiny, and through scrutiny eventually to control. This was an intense and rigorous learning experience for the students; continued over time they developed a high level of physical control and awareness. It was this work, which began in the Vieux-Colombier School and continued as part of the training regime for Les Copiaus, which the young student Etienne Decroux was later to transform into his corporeal mime technique. It was the clarity, skill and precision of this work which also facilitated the international success of the Vieux-Colombier company, and of its later off-shoots Les Copiaus and the Compagnie des Quinze.

THE ACTOR AND THE MASK

From the mid-nineteenth century onwards there was a steady revival of interest in the mask as a channel for dramatic expression, rather than as a decorative symbol (Eldredge 1996: 12). The theatrical mask was strongly associated with the classical Greek and Roman theatre, and with the Italian commedia dell'arte, all of which were growing in popularity as a result of changes in cultural taste and advances in scholarship. The re-emergence of the mask as an expressive tool may mark a cultural nostalgia for the idea of a society more closely in touch with its deep motive forces. Sears Eldredge (ibid.: 13) also suggests that the use of the mask within the creative arts during this period was linked to wider intellectual currents generated by the work of psychologists Sigmund Freud (1856–1939) and Carl Jung (1875–1961). The possibility of using the mask to liberate the creative subconscious meant that the performer could explore deeper connections with the primitive, the ritualistic and the sacred, taping into powerful energies and engaging with themes central to much early twentieth-century cultural activity (see Innes 1993): 'The mask exteriorises a deep aspect of life, and in so doing, it helps to rediscover instinct' (Barrault 1961: 76–7). This regenerative expressive power, together with the mask's strong association with theatre forms which were vigorous and energetic (commedia dell'arte), holy and/or sacred (African and Ancient Greek), and ritualised and exotic (Asian–Nōh, Topeng, Kabuki) helped to position it as both culturally powerful and creatively nourishing.

Both before and after the First World War, a wide range of artists (**Alfred Jarry**, Vsevelod Meyerhold, **W. B. Yeats**, Edward Gordon Craig, **Luigi Pirandello**, **Oskar Schlemmer**, and the **German Expressionists** to name but a few) found inspiration in the mask – valuing both its use in training and its effects in performance.

Edward Gordon Craig pronounced in his influential journal, *The Mask*, that:

> The mask must return to the stage to restore expression ... the visible expression
> of the mind ... the inspiration which led man to use the mask in past ages is the

same now as it ever was and will never die. It is this inspiration that we shall act under and in which we trust.

(John Balance [Edward Gordon Craig] 1908: 11)

Craig also experimented with masks in the training he offered at his School for the Art of the Theatre at the Arena Goldini in Florence, including work on the techniques of the commedia dell'arte. No doubt Copeau knew of some of these international experiments, and perhaps he recalled Craig's work and writings as he drew up his initial ideas for the Vieux-Colombier.

For many artists the First World War represented the outcome of a terrible and violent breach between humankind's inner psychological and outer political worlds. The mask offered both a metaphor for the expression of this disjuncture and a means for healing and renewal:

After the First World War, when all the old values collapsed with the empires and traditional ideas, the search went on for the forgotten primitive forms and sources which were resurrected in basic modern dance, in the volcanic stammering cries of Expressionistic despair, in the Dadaistic fury of self-defiance, and in the phantasmagoric Surrealism with its glazing of Freudian imagery. The mask returned, reflecting and revealing the savage instinct of man let loose again, the old demonic spirits in new clothing, the spirits man feared and tried to escape while falling prey to them. The mask triumphed in leading man back to its cruel sources and projecting its influence with a sophisticated gesture, often hiding as a mask behind non-masklike masks.

(Sorell 1973: 15)

During this period the mask came to represent not simply the savage chaos of untamed human nature, but it developed as an expressive tool with which to explore what was increasingly recognised as the fluid, transformative and multi-faceted nature of modern human identity. Copeau's experiments came at a time and in a place when cultural tastes allowed them to flourish. His work was significantly less subject to interruptions and to interference from political opponents than the work of some of his international colleagues.

Thomas Leabhart (who studied with Etienne Decroux from 1968 to 1972) argues that the mask also fulfils a shamanic function within Copeau's work (Leabhart 1995). He identifies the frequent use of metaphors of possession and altered states of consciousness in Copeau's writings on mask improvisation as an indicator of this function. The mask is, he suggests, a symbol for the experience many actors have of being taken over by some quality during performance which changes their level of consciousness. In Copeau's theatre the mask could operate holistically, rather than politically, to heal the division between the actor's body and will – releasing the body into controlled and yet spontaneous physical expression of the actor's creativity. The mask was, in this sense, a method by which the actor could re-establish the vitality of the theatre, its primitive life-blood restored once more to its veins. For Copeau, the magic of the theatre was based on its physical truths, on the corporeal power and technique of the actor. He was less enthusiastic about symbolic and abstract uses of the mask, and as a result his work did not suffer when such usage went out of fashion after the outbreak of the Second World War. Copeau's fascination with both the past and the future is perfectly encapsulated by the mask – it embodies the insights of a distant but vital past, and is at the same time forever of the present, plastic and complex, representative of the duality and complexity of the human nature with which it is intimately linked.

At the time when Copeau began to use masks in his training exercises, such exercises were revolutionary and 'totally exceptional' (Leabhart 1995: 90). Copeau's first sustained experiments with the mask as a training instrument took place in December 1921. The students' initial explorations focussed on the manufacture of the mask. Copeau had started by covering the students' faces with a handkerchief or a stocking, but students soon progressed to using cardboard, papier-mâché, shellac and flour, and linen and glue (Kusler 1979: 30). Eventually a sculptor, Albert Marque, taught the students better methods of construction and design, enabling the achievement of the neutral effect which Copeau sought: 'Without Albert Marque, we would have continued to make masks "small and pretty". A good mask must be neutral; its expression depends on your movements' (Dorcy 1961: 13).

THE NEUTRAL OR NOBLE MASK

Copeau's own life experience convinced him of the value and importance of starting from the simplest place possible. He had built his success as an actor, writer, teacher and director from nothing more than his rigorous commitment to paring away that which was unnecessary and seeking out the living impulses which demanded expression. The tool that Copeau used to assist his students in achieving this condition was the neutral mask. The neutral mask draws together many of the elements of Copeau's teaching, and the principles of its use also underpin his theatre work with both the Vieux-Colombier and Les Copiaus. The aim of the neutral mask is to 'depersonalise' the student actor, 'stripping away the idiosyncratic movement or behaviour that is "you"' (Eldredge 1996: 50). In this manner, the students are removed from the 'everyday' world, and from an uncritical acceptance of their psychophysical self. From this point of self-recognition they are then able to rebuild themselves towards dramatic characterisation, their transformation made more secure through the conscious paring away of unnecessary social habits: 'The actor would have to be stripped as bare as the stage; only then could he express himself clearly and simply' (Eldredge and Huston 1995: 121).

As those who have used it can testify, the neutral mask gives the wearer a very special experience of their action, one of Copeau's students described the mask as conveying 'a power and unknown security – a sort of balance and consciousness of each gesture and of oneself' (Kusler 1979: 30). This physical self-knowledge gives the actor the confidence of knowing where they are starting from, what Copeau describes as: 'The point of departure of an expression. The state of repose, of calm, of relaxation or decontraction, of silence or simplicity' (Copeau in Rudlin 1986: 46). The student learns, through their body, the simplicity and internal dynamics of effective theatre communication:

> An actor must know how to be silent, to listen, respond, keep still, begin a gesture, develop it, return to stillness and to silence, with all the tones and half-tones that those actions imply.
>
> (Ibid.)

With the help of the sculptor Albert Marque, Copeau's students explored the construction of 'neutral' or 'noble' masks, each making their own perfectly-fitting mask. The mask was originally referred to as 'noble' in reference to the expressionless masks worn by eighteenth century aristocrats in order to preserve their anonymity (Murray 2003: 31), however the term 'neutral' conveys the mask's purpose more effectively and without the misleading associations. The mask aims to remove from the students the temptation to 'act' and return them to a state of intuitive understanding based on simple physical engagement with the world around them. The mask helps the actor to simplify and sustain the gesture, it helps them also to find 'interior inspiration' (Copeau in Rudlin 1986: 48) and to find a new simpler authenticity in the students' acting.

POPULAR FORMS OF THEATRE: ANCIENT, MODERN AND SACRED

> [P]rogress is not always a step forward
>
> (Copeau 1990: 165)

The third main theme informing Copeau's work is the role of popular and sacred theatre within a modern society. Although Copeau's work is often positioned alongside the theatre of the European avant garde and intellectual elite, this is to misrepresent his aims and achievements. His mission to rejuvenate French theatre, motivated by his passionate dislike of the commercialised boulevard theatres, was intended to do more than just convulse what the Parisian intellectual elite saw as a cultural corpse into new life. Likewise, his innovations in the training of professional actors were also intended to do more than simply improve the standard of acting. Copeau's aims were far more profound and wide-reaching.

He constantly denied that he sought in any way to anticipate the theatre of the future:

> There is no drama of the future. Drama is essentially a fact of the present, a contemporary phenomenon, a proposition whose destiny depends on the reception and the response given to it.
>
> (Copeau 1990: 188).

Nonetheless, he dreamed of the possibility that theatre might regain the socially unifying and spiritually regenerative power that he believed it once possessed during the great periods of theatre history (Ancient Greece, Medieval Europe and Japan, Renaissance Europe), and to this end he strove throughout his life to prepare the way for such a renaissance. He struggled to hold down his ticket prices to a level that he hoped would not deter those living and working in the *quartier*. His productions strove to maintain an intimate and open relationship between stage and auditorium to encourage a shared experience between both. What Copeau so admired about the popular theatres of the past was that they had discovered theatrical forms which enabled the people to engage with something more profound than frivolous entertainment, or even the social or political issues of the day; they touched on the very nature of human existence. Theatre, for Copeau, should 'originate in the moral life of the people' (Copeau 1990: 188), bringing to life the deep and profound forces which shape human existence and our understanding of it, in a theatrical form which all could appreciate. Copeau's search for a theatre that might speak to all the people was driven by several deeply personal convictions: his belief in the value of theatre as a collaborative act; his desire to re-unite the heart and the head of both the performer and the spectator; his respect for the great theatre of the past and for the young writers of today; his recognition of the dangerous myopia of a theatre culture based almost entirely on the cosmopolitan tastes of the capital city; and, his religious convictions – particularly during his later years. In 1941, Copeau wrote a seminal article which set out his views on the nature and importance of popular theatre, 'Le Théâtre Populaire' (important sections are translated in Copeau 1990: 186–95). In part this article is a veiled response to the German Occupation of France, but it is also an attempt to explain how he saw the historical development of theatre's social and moral role. It is valuable to examine some of the issues thrown up by this article.

WHAT IS POPULAR THEATRE?

> What the French call 'Théâtre Populaire' ... does not mean 'popular theatre' in the sense of frothy comedies which would have a broad appeal to the most frivolous public. *Théâtre populaire* is theatre for the *people*, *le peuple*, the working man, the masses.
>
> (Leonard Pronko in Copeau 1990: 182)

European popular theatre developed rapidly in the early days of the twentieth century as social and cultural reforms encouraged greater democracy both inside and outside the theatre. It is a broad and general concept, encompassing several other theatrical trends, which sought to extend the theatrical event to all levels of society: the elite, the leisured classes, the bourgeoisie and the working class. Popular theatre has taken several directions: religious theatre, political theatre, decentralised and touring theatre, and community theatre (Bradby and McCormick 1978: 13); all of which sought in their own way to challenge the theatrical conventions of the day, breaking down those practices which inhibited the relationship between the stage and people.

The development of 'popular theatre' in the early twentieth century was closely related to the (re)negotiation of general unifying concepts of the 'people'. In Revolutionary Russia, Marxist theories of the people-as-proletariat provided a rationale for a 'popular theatre' which began with agit-prop and ended with socialist realism. In Weimar Germany, a politically and economically destabilised society swung from socialism and expressionism towards the totalitarianism and mass rallies of the National Socialists and the Third Reich. While France did not experience the same painful upheavals as Russia or Germany, nonetheless its cultural identity was split and fractured in other ways. The political uncertainty caused by the Franco-Prussian War, the terrible losses of the First World War, and later the German Occupation during the Second World War, all created a need for a theatre that could heal divisions and confirm the value of French culture. Copeau believed that, by decentralising and discovering a theatre language that was direct, sincere, committed and engaging, drama could participate in the regeneration of a vital and inclusive national cultural identity: 'it will be a very simple, direct form, saying only what it has to say, clearly, to everyone, and concerned with their real-life pre-occupations' (Copeau 1990: 182–3).

In his search for a new form of French popular theatre, Copeau was drawn towards examples both past and present for inspiration. He felt instinctively that some element of what he was looking for was present in the great Ancient Greek dramas, in medieval mystery plays, in the commedia dell'arte; as well as in music, in the work of family circus acts such as the Fratellini Brothers, and even in the cinema antics of **Charlie Chaplin**, all of which he understood as in some profound sense linked.

Charlie Chaplin (1889–1977) was an English-born film actor and director. He began his career as a child performer, eventually settling in America where he became a pioneer of early silent-movie comedy. He played his trade-mark character, the 'little tramp' in over seventy films, to huge popular acclaim. Copeau and Chaplin met in Paris. Copeau went with Chaplin to the circus and recalled the immense popularity of Chaplin with the public: 'I saw the whole crowd get up, from top to bottom of the stands and, with one movement, 3000 people surged into the ring and crowded round the little actor' (Copeau 1990: 184). Chaplin's 'little tramp', though over-sentimental to today's tastes, demonstrated for Copeau the possibility of discovering meaningful modern character types which had popular appeal, and confirmed the value of an agile physicality for the contemporary actor.

He believed that theatre would be popular only if it was 'living', and conversely that theatre could only find vitality through an engagement with the people and their experience. At the Volta Congress in 1934, Copeau responded to the revolutionary passion of the Russian delegate, Alexander Taïrov, by suggesting that:

> The question is not in knowing whether today's theatre will draw its appeal from this or that experimentation, its strength from the authority of one director or another: I think we must ask ourselves whether it will be Marxist or Christian. For it must be living, that is to say, popular. To be living, it must give man reasons to believe, to hope, to grow.
>
> (Copeau 1990: 189)

Copeau was not a Marxist, but his words suggest that he was able to understand what was of importance and value in the work of his fellow

Russian theatre artists. Both he and Taïrov believed that theatre has to redefine itself in relation to the needs of the society within which it functions, and that it needs to reconnect with a popular audience. Copeau was, in effect, seeking to redefine popular theatre as a form distinct from that theatre which simply attracts a mass audience. This could be seen as a form of cultural elitism, a claim to know what is best for the people, what they really need, but Copeau is careful to insist that the new forms he sought should grow out of the needs of the people and be rooted in their experience. His particular ambition was to look beyond the needs of the urban and industrialised population of Paris, towards a notion of popular theatre which also acknowledged the culture and life experiences of the people of the rural regions.

MODELS FOR A NEW POPULAR THEATRE

[W]e must destroy existing forms and return to primitive forms.
(Ariane Mnouchkine quoting Copeau in Bradby and Williams 1988: 96)

Copeau knew that the answer did not lie in staging endless historical revivals, however authentically presented. He saw nothing but danger in 'behaving like sight-seers or dilettantes in love with a lost art form' (Copeau 1990: 153). Nonetheless he did hope that it might be possible to heal a fragmented secular society by returning to theatre forms which could tap into the spiritual power of the religious ritual and the communal joy of the improvised comedy. New or renewed forms were needed if the popular audience was to be drawn away from the commercially successful melodramas, circuses, fairgrounds and cinemas towards his dream of a vibrant, popular theatre that could speak to a wide constituency and deal with profound subject matters. Copeau believed that such forms would be 'living' because: 'they will have grown out of the people for whom they were made, they will have been renewed, refreshed at the very source, and will have developed organically, naturally' (ibid.: 195). Two particular models seem to have most inspired Copeau: the commedia dell'arte and the medieval mystery play.

Commedia dell'arte

Aim for nothing less than making the actor, not only the medium, but the source of all dramatic inspiration.

(Copeau 1990: 12)

Copeau's ultimate aim, throughout his various projects, was to build a company of creative actors – a company with a clear sense of purpose, a solid workmanlike base in technique and skills, an *esprit de corps*, and a sense of self-sufficiency (Copeau 1990: 47). This was one of the primary aims of the School, and, Copeau believed, an important means of achieving a revitalised theatre – a theatre in which actors can be 'left entirely to their own devices, as creators and workers' (ibid.). Following the example of Molière, he looked to the traditions of the Italian commedia dell'arte for encouragement and ideas. He had clearly been intrigued and enthused by commedia dell'arte from as early as the 1917 production of *Les Fourberies de Scapin*. Over the next few years he planned for a brotherhood of actors who would work and create together, exploring the possibility of a new commedia, but it is not until the retreat to Burgundy in 1924 that he was able to explore fully potential models for the creation of a 'new comedy'. The new form was not to be a straightforward re-creation of commedia and its stock characters (Harlequin, Colombine, Pantalone, Brighella, the Captain and others), but rather an attempt to develop new characters for a new age. In Copeau's plan, each actor, 'would henceforth dedicate themselves almost entirely to improvisation' (Copeau in Rudlin 1986: 96). The relationship between the actor and the character they played would be extended and intimate – they would be required to:

> Fatten it from the substance of their own being, identify with it, think of it at all times, live with it, giving things to it, not only from his own personality, external mannerisms and physical peculiarities, but also from his own way of feeling, of thinking, his temperament, his outlook, his experience, letting it profit from his reading, as well as growing and changing with him.
>
> (Ibid.)

The skills, techniques and traditions associated with the medieval booth player enjoyed a period of renewed popularity in the early decades of the century. Artists of all kinds – Picasso, Meyerhold, Craig, Schoenberg, Stravinsky, and Chaplin – were fascinated by the vitality of forms such as the commedia dell'arte, the circus, and the fairground, and the opportunities they offered to combine energy and emotion in new and popular ways. For Copeau, these opportunities transposed themselves into: introducing his student-actors to the acrobatic and clowning skills of the circus; encouraging them to create their own characters and scenarios, using song, music and dance as well as drama; and developing his mask-training exercises to include the half-mask. Les Copiaus responded to the new challenges with enthusiasm and imagination. Each company member developed a character of their own, one of the most successful being Michel Saint-Denis' character, Oscar Knie. Knie grew from some left-over costume items (an old coat and some baggy trousers), a stick and an old piece of rolled-up carpet; his mask based on Saint-Denis' instinctual understanding of the character, and his observations of real people. Rudlin notes that the majority of the characters created for the 'new comedy' were male (1986: 104), and suggests that the processes which Copeau set up for the masked improvisations were competitive, and favoured those willing to be assertive, those willing to lose themselves in the mask, and those able to cope with the physical demands of prolonged masked improvisation. Perhaps the lack of female role models from the original commedia dell'arte was also a factor – the only parts for women tended to be lovers and maids, all of whom were unmasked.

The success of Copeau's search for a 'new comedy' was limited. His young actors worked hard to develop the necessary skills, but some were inevitably more successful than others, and it proved particularly difficult to create dialogue of the same quality as the physical improvisations. Several productions by the Copiaus company did manage to show what might be possible with time, resources and training – Copeau's adaptation of *L'Illusion* (from original texts by Fernando de Rojas and Pierre Corneille), first performed in 1926; and, *La Danse de la Ville et des Champs* (scenario by Michel Saint-Denis and Jean Villard-Gilles), first performed in 1928 (see Rudlin 1986: 105–10 for details) – but by the end of the decade Copeau and his young protégés had parted company, and the search for a 'new comedy' had effectively passed into the hands of the next generation.

Mystery plays and open-air spectacles

Copeau's notebooks for 1915 record Craig's enthusiasm for the ancient ceremonies performed in the squares of Florence: 'That is theatre, that is what I should like to do – let the cities give me full freedom to organise beautiful outdoor spectacles like that' (Craig in Copeau 1990: 17). This vision seems to have stayed with Copeau for the next twenty or so years, until, in the later years of his life, he was able to mount a small number of

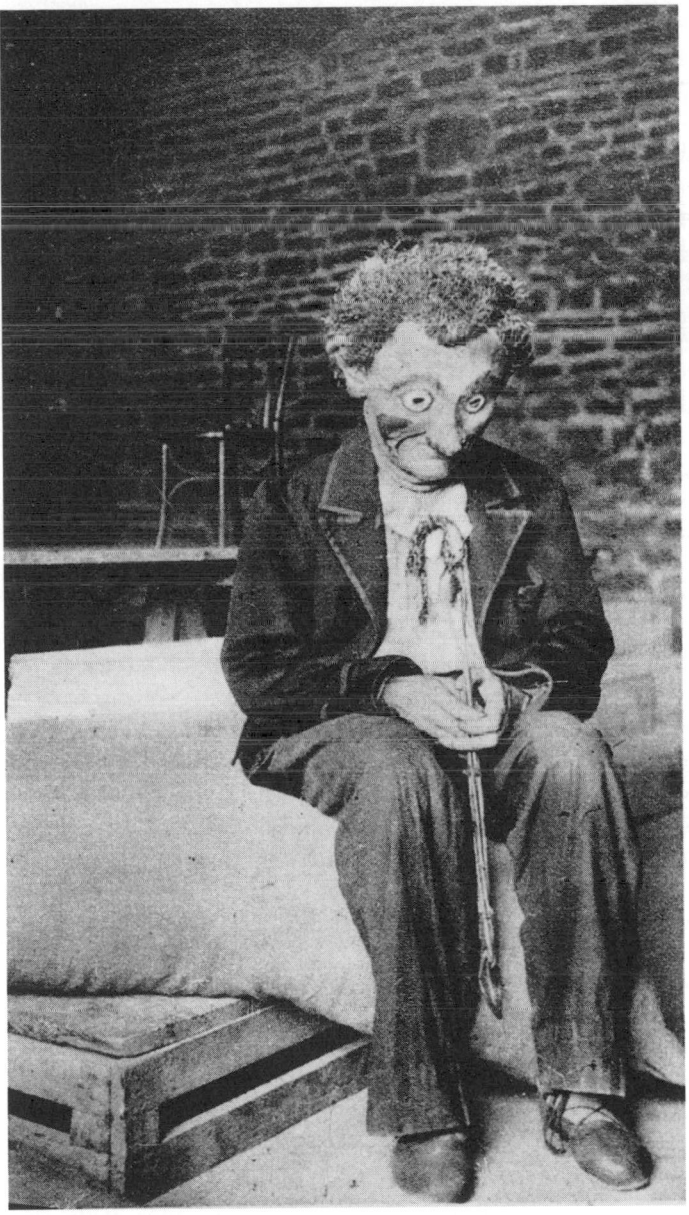

Figure 2.2 Michel Saint-Denis as M. Knie, rehearsing for *L'Illusion* (1926)

religious mystery plays in the open air in Florence, and in Beaune. He had experimented with open air performance before – rehearsing at Limon, presenting *Les Fourberies de Scapin* in the Place Saint-Sulpice, rehearsing and performing in the open air with Les Copiaus in Burgundy – but never on the kind of scale available to him for these spectacles. His move towards the religious mystery play as a popular theatre form was also informed by his late conversion to Catholicism. It concerned Copeau that the acting profession itself was capable of exerting a negative spiritual influence, perverting the student actor's integrity through the necessity to live a pretence. His religious convictions left him feeling increasingly ambivalent about his chosen profession – as he wrote in 1929, at the time of the disbanding of Les Copiaus, 'the actor is doing something forbidden: he is playing with his humanness and making sport of it' (Copeau in Rudlin 2000: 58). He could no longer rely on his students to commit to his semi-monastic vision of life in the theatre – yet he still yearned for the kind of communion, of letting-go-of-the-self, which theatre provided and which increasingly informed his personal beliefs. The revival of religious drama across Europe in the middle of the twentieth century sprang not just from the rediscovery of the morality plays and mystery plays of the Middle Ages but also from the sense of spiritual and moral decay which many felt as a result of the two World Wars. Even such an anarchic figure as Antonin Artaud can be seen as representing the same desire for a renewed connection between theatre, the self, and society. Artaud's search for a spiritually rejuvenating theatre is a more extreme version of Copeau's, but it also seeks to exploit the same use of a more directly shared space to bring together large numbers of people for profound spiritual events. A desire for communion and spiritual redemption may have been something which drew Copeau towards what he saw as a purer, less morally degenerate form of theatre.

Some have suggested that Copeau's Catholicism and his (perceived) cultural nostalgia for the theatre of the past might leave him a little too close to the ritualistic representations of a greater power central to European fascism (Ward 1996: 180). Copeau's critique of the Nazi rally (Copeau 1990: 194) does indeed focus more on form than content, but it is hard to blame him for being circumspect given the dangers of overt criticism during the German Occupation. It is quite clear that Copeau does not see such 'grandiose' events as in anyway falling within the domain of popular theatre. Furthermore, it is hard to believe that someone who set so much store by individuality, imagination and simple, moral integrity would be in any way seduced by the bombast of the Nazi mass rally.

POPULAR THEATRE: POLICY AND DECENTRALISATION

In *Le Théâtre populaire* (1941), Copeau foresaw the development of a new concept of national theatre – decentralised, popular and youthful. At the time that he was writing, young companies had already started to emerge around France, initially supported by subsidies from the Popular Front government of the 1930s, and later scattered by the German Occupation. The move away from Paris was in this sense both a move towards regional audiences of working people, and a move away from the centre of Nazi control over France. As far as conventional theatre was concerned, 'The little live drama available to provincials was provided by tours of the previous Parisian season's commercial successes or small touring companies, often of semi-amateur status'(Bradby 1984: 87). After the Second World War, the new Socialist government saw an opportunity to re-unite the country through providing support to theatre in the regions. Another important political and cultural model was the French Resistance; the German Occupation of Paris had meant that its operational control was spread out across the country, and that its cultural resistance focused on regional needs. The Ministry of Education supported the establishment, in 1947, of two Centres Dramatiques (Drama Centres): one was set up in Strasbourg, and was eventually run by Michel Saint-Denis; the other in Saint-Etienne by Jean Dasté. Several other of Copeau's former colleagues also made important contributions to the decentralisation of French theatre; Léon Chancerel, for instance, founded the Comédiens Routiers in association with the Scout movement in the decade before the War. In this way, government interest in the cultural development of the regions and the commitment of Copeau's young disciples to a decentralised theatre found a happy meeting ground. Since the War, the French government has continued to encourage decentralisation through the creation of further Centres Dramatiques and Maisons de la Culture (Arts Centres), and the support of new writing, touring theatre work, as well as the support of regional festivals (such as the Festival at Avignon). The appointment in 1951 of Jean Vilar, who had founded the Avignon Festival, as the director of the Théâtre Nationale

Populaire at the Chaillot Palace across the river from the Eiffel Tower meant that the cultural aesthetics and the politics of this popular theatre movement finally also came to the doorsteps of the Paris elite.

For Copeau, decentralisation did not simply mean taking Parisian theatre to the regions, it involved the development of centres for regional theatrical development. At the heart of each regional centre's work, Copeau envisaged a programme of training, run by expert teachers, to explore and practice 'all forms of dramatic invention and performance' (Copeau 1990: 191). Further, the necessity for these young companies of 'travelling light' enforced a reduction of 'baggage', so that 'the sobriety of the *mise en scène* is accepted as one of their characteristics' (ibid.: 192). Jean Dasté insisted that his company in Saint-Etienne toured with only one vehicle into which everything (props, set, costume and actors) must fit (Bradby 1984: 89). Copeau's excitement at the prospect of these young companies is almost palpable: they are unfettered by 'the discipline of routine, pedantic and unimaginative criticism' (Copeau 1990: 192), free from the constraints of Naturalism, alive to the possibilities of mime and lyricism, and convinced of the need to create their own repertoire. This was a powerful and compelling vision for the time, generous and alive to the needs of the country as a whole and the energies of the young artists of the future. The measure of the importance of Copeau's vision can be read in the distance it has travelled. In post-War Britain for example, the development of regional repertory theatres, some with Theatre-in-Education and Community departments attached to their main house work (e.g. Coventry's Belgrade Theatre); the establishment of regional drama schools such as Bristol Old Vic Theatre School (originally intended to be linked to the Old Vic School in London, led by Michel Saint-Denis); and the encouragement of innovative touring companies and of new writing (Joan Littlewood's Theatre Workshop, and the English Stage Company at the Royal Court), can all be seen as echoing the spirit of Copeau's vision. Ultimately, Copeau understood the essential fact that for any theatre to be a national art form it was necessary for it to be a popular art form; and, that in order to achieve both, it must be allowed to develop its own relationship with the people, to find its own reasons for being. The old social rituals of theatre-going – evening dress, expensive programmes and long intervals – had more to do with class than the real value of the theatre event, which at the end of the day resided in the nature and the quality of the communication between stage and auditorium.

3

COPEAU'S IDEAS IN PRODUCTION – *LES FOURBERIES DE SCAPIN*

Jacques Copeau recognised that a renewed French theatre could not and should not blindly turn its back on the past. To do so would be to ignore the vital energies and the powerful sense of scenic poetry which he believed informed the work of the great dramatic authors. Throughout the most productive phases of his career, Copeau brought the same experimental rigour to his revivals of classic plays as he did to the work of new French playwrights. In fact, it would be fair to say that a large part of his reputation as a powerful force in French and European theatre was based on his revivals of works by classic playwrights such as Shakespeare and Molière. In some respects the motivation for Copeau in mounting revivals was clearer and more immediate. For over two hundred years, the **Comédie-Française** had regarded itself as the 'spiritual home' of Molière and the classic French dramatists, Copeau was to attempt nothing less than a full-scale assault on this cultural dominance.

This chapter will examine a key production from one of the most productive periods of Copeau's career. Between *Une Femme Tuée par la Douceur (A Woman Killed with Kindness)* in 1913 and his departure for Burgundy in 1924, the Vieux-Colombier Theatre, under Copeau's direction, produced something in the region of 147 productions (including revivals). Such a large and varied body of work makes the task of picking one production very difficult. Several of his productions (e.g. *La*

The **Comédie-Française** is the national theatre of France, and the oldest national theatre in the world. Founded after Molière's death in 1673, it has survived several historical crises which have seen it divide and re-unite. Its reputation is based largely on its productions of classic French playwrights such as Molière, Racine and Corneille, though it has also produced notable productions of modern writers. The director-ship of the Comédie-Française is a state appointment; the post was briefly held by Copeau in 1940.

Nuit des Rois (Twelfth Night), *Les Frères Karamazov (The Brothers Karamazov)*, and *Le Pacquebot (Tenacity)* are already covered in some detail elsewhere (Kurtz 1999, Rudlin 1986). Equally not all of his productions with the Vieux-Colombier give us useful insights into his later work in Burgundy. Copeau was never closely associated with any one particular contemporary playwright, as Stanislavsky was with Anton Chekhov for instance; however, if there was one constant lodestar guiding Copeau's career it was Molière. Molière's life and work, as we have already seen, represented so much of what Copeau aspired to achieve within a living, artistic and socially purposeful theatre. Copeau produced most of Molière's plays at some point during his career, but one production in particular can be seen as central in the development of his ideas and practices, the late comedy *Les Fourberies de Scapin (The Tricks of Scapin)*. The play was first performed by the Vieux-Colombier company in the Garrick Theatre in New York on 27 November 1917 and remained in the repertoire until 13 May 1922, when it was presented in the open air outside the Church of Saint-Sulpice in Paris; the production's four and a half year life-span thus encompasses probably the most productive and critically successful period for both Copeau and his company. It is during this period that Copeau is able to realise for the first time many of his most cherished ambitions: the secure commencement of the Vieux-Colombier School, the nurturing of new theatrical talent, the development of improvisation within rehearsal and training, the use of masks in training, and the exploration of the skills and traditions of the Italian commedia dell'arte. *Les Fourberies de Scapin* provides us with an insight into the significant links between Copeau's work in direction and performance and his ideas for the rejuvenation of the theatre. There is certainly much of interest in the later work of Les Copiaus; but the work after 1924, whilst it reflects Copeau's visionary influence, relies less on his own personal contribution. Adequate records, reviews, photographs and testimonies survive for Copeau's productions of *Les Fourberies de Scapin* to enable us to examine the production in sufficient detail – in particular Louis Jouvet's carefully annotated edition of the play (Molière 1951) provides details of some of Copeau's original stage directions and represents perhaps the closest we can get to a textual recreation of one of his productions.

LES FOURBERIES DE SCAPIN (THE TRICKS OF SCAPIN) BY MOLIÈRE

In 1920 Copeau gave a production of *Les Fourberies de Scapin* by Molière. Set on a bare platform, ruthlessly lit like a boxing ring, it recaptured the spirit of the Commedia dell'Arte without any laborious imitation of the past.

(Saint-Denis 1960: 22)

Les Fourberies de Scapin is one of Molière's late three-act farces; it was first performed in Paris at the Palais Royal (the home of Molière's company) in 1671, two years before his death. At first sight it seems a strange choice for Copeau to mount a revival of such a light piece at the start of such an important event as the Vieux-Colombier's first season in New York, but the play was chosen for two very specific purposes. On the one hand, the play represented a piece of cultural propaganda; it was intended to warm the American audience to the French people – the performance was introduced by Suzanne Bing, who greeted the audience, offering 'a smile from France in the midst of war' (Bing in Kurtz 1999: 53). Bing's greeting was followed by an introduction in which each member of the company announced their name and responsibility. Copeau was very aware of the need to explain what the company were about to present – its relationship to their work as a whole, and to the principles underpinning their performances. On the other hand, the production represented a return to the basics of theatre and acting; Copeau's own statement reveals his commitment to the search for what is direct, simple and self-renewing in theatre: 'I am simply a man who performs his job as best he can, learning it each day, and each day discovering something he did not know the day before' (Copeau in Kurtz 1999: 53). This statement is on one level offered as a simple gesture of modest humility in front of a new audience, but we can also read it as an indication of the 'attitude' with which Copeau intended that the play should be performed. Acting was a serious job – a task that the actor had to undertake 'as best he can' – and the work should be undertaken with as little fuss as possible. It was the duty of the actors therefore to apply themselves whole-heartedly to the task of embodying the characters' actions, without embellishment. Furthermore, the actors should pour their interest into what they were doing, absorb themselves in the task – the process of acting thus became a journey for the actor, and the art of acting was always coming into knowledge and never fully achieved.

In much the same way that Shakespeare had, by this time, become iconic within British theatre, Molière had also acquired a similar status within the French theatre. Copeau's production broke away from the reverential and tired traditions of the Comédie-Française to present the play with a vigour, physicality and playfulness which critics had not experienced before – 'Molière reborn!' exclaimed one reviewer (John Corbin, *The Times*, 2 December 1917). What Copeau possessed was an ability to draw out of his actors performances which *embodied* the words and made physically present the energies, rhythms and playfulness of the text. However despite the production's originality, Copeau was adamant that he was not so much revolutionising theatre as rediscovering its essential principles. To make this clear he declared that 'This production of *Les Fourberies* is in the traditional category, it is not revolutionary' (Copeau in Molière 1951: 21, author's translation).

The Vieux-Colombier's first production of the play met with a generally positive reception in New York. Audience numbers were smaller than expected, perhaps because the piece was considered too light and farce too insignificant a medium for an audience who had come expecting something more weighty and profound. Most critics were intrigued and amused by the play's staging, fascinated by the *tréteau nu*, and engaged by the cast's playfulness and directness. Copeau's atmospheric and emotionally intense adaptation of Dostoyevsky's novel, *Les Frères Karamazov (The Brothers Karamazov)*, which was revived a few months later, did better box office – it was more in line with the popular tastes of the New York theatre-going public. Nonetheless, *Les Fourberies de Scapin* offers an important illustration of the kind of actor-based theatre which Copeau had advocated so strongly during his lecture tour the previous winter: 'Here was a play acted with the body far more than with the brain or the voice' (Kurtz 1999: 53). The production was woven through with a simplicity, freshness, imagination and vigour which must have been a pleasant surprise to any for whom Molière had become little more than an historical figure or a 'national treasure'.

Copeau's belief in the play and its importance in relation to the company's mission was not shaken by the reaction in New York. He decided to restage *Les Fourberies de Scapin* as part of the company's new season on their return to Paris. No doubt he wished to reassert his personal belief in the production, and also perhaps to fine tune it in more sympathetic surroundings. The Paris critics were more receptive to his innovations, though their comments still betrayed a lingering scepticism that the piece was significant enough to merit Copeau's attention. What the critics missed was the value of Copeau's work for the working-class theatre-goer. Maurice Kurtz relates how Georges Vitray, one of Copeau's actors, overheard a worker express to a friend his amazement, after seeing *Les Fourberies*, that, '*mon vieux*, you know what? They don't have stage sets. They sit right on the steps so you *see the words*' (cited in Kurtz 1999: 84). What better expression could there be of Copeau's special talent for making the text come alive with a physical presence. *Les Fourberies de Scapin* was also an important production for Copeau's own personal creative journey. It marked a key stage in his exploration of the skills and techniques of the commedia dell'arte, an exploration which was to culminate in the 'new Commedia' created by Les Copiaus. It introduced the *tréteau nu* (bare platform) which Copeau borrowed from the medieval theatre, as a central element in a simple and uncluttered staging system. Equally, the open-air performance of the play in May 1922, in the Place Saint-Sulpice in the Latin Quarter of Paris, can be seen in hindsight as a pre-cursor of the 'booth' theatre performances of Les Copiaus and of the public pageantry of Copeau's later sacred plays.

THE PLAY: A SYNOPSIS OF THE PLOT

Les Fourberies de Scapin is a three act prose comedy, set in Naples. Below is an outline of the plot:

Act 1

The young Octavio panics when he hears the news from his valet Sylvestre that his father, Argante, is returning, eager to marry him off to Hyacinthe, the absent daughter of his old friend Géronte. In despair

Octavio turns to Scapin for advice and help. He describes the situation to Scapin, explaining his friend Léandre's love for a young gypsy girl, Zerbinette, and his own affections for another poor young woman, whom he has only just married three days ago. The young woman, who unbeknown to Octavio is actually Géronte's daughter Hyacinthe, enters and they both proclaim their undying love for each other. Scapin agrees to help the lovers, he starts by teaching Octavio how to stand up to his father's questioning. Despite Scapin's tutoring, Octavio runs off as his father enters, leaving Scapin and Sylvestre to face the wrath of Argante, who has just heard of his son's marriage to an unknown girl. Scapin argues that Octavio was forced into marriage by the young woman's family, plotting that Argante will forgive his son if he thinks that he was simply unfortunate enough to be 'caught out'. Nonetheless Argante threatens that the marriage must be annulled, despite Scapin's appeals to the damage that might be done to his own and his son's reputation. Scapin has begun to lay his plot and now recruits Sylvestre as a player in his scheme.

Act 2

Argante and Géronte bicker with each other over the cause of the problems besetting their marriage plans for their off-spring, blaming each other's bad parenting. Argante leaves having hinted that Géronte should look to the behaviour of his own son, Léandre. Léandre enters and is confronted by his father who, before he leaves for his house, demands to know the truth about what has gone on. On meeting Octavio and Scapin, Léandre accuses his valet of betraying him. He threatens Scapin with a beating unless he owns up to what he has done – Scapin owns up to several misdemeanours, but not to telling Géronte about Léandre's romance. Carlo, a rascal, enters and tells Léandre that gypsies have his beloved Zerbinette and that unless he pays them at once he will lose her forever. Léandre now has to beg Scapin to help him out, and Scapin makes him take back all the names and insults he has just been called before he agrees to help both Octavio and Léandre raise the cash they need to solve their problems. Scapin then tells the two lovers to fetch Sylvestre while he engages with Argante, who is still determined to get his son's marriage annulled. Scapin lies that the family of Octavio's wife are willing to fix a quick annulment for a large sum of money. Scapin, wheedles and connives, trying everything to get Argante to agree to pay the sum Octavio requires, two hundred pounds. Sylvestre enters, disguised as a villainous member of the wife's family, and hearing from Scapin of Argante's reluctance to pay up threatens to kill him. Argante, terrified, hides behind Scapin and listens and watches as the disguised Sylvestre shows how Argante will die when he finds him. This convinces Argante, who, as soon as Sylvestre has left, gives Scapin the money. Scapin then turns his attention to Géronte, pretending to search desperately for him in order to let him know that his son has been kidnapped by sailors from a Turkish galley who are demanding five hundred guineas in ransom. Géronte too falls for Scapin's tricks and, reluctantly, hands over the money. Scapin gives the money to the two lovers and swears to get his revenge on Géronte for the way he has treated him.

Act 3

Hyacinthe and Zerbinette are brought together for safety, under the care of Sylvestre and Scapin. Zerbinette expresses her resolution that she shall not return Léandre's love until she is sure of his hand in marriage. Zerbinette tells Hyacinthe that she does not know who her parents are. Scapin suggests that it is the ups and downs of love and life that make both enjoyable. The others go off leaving Scapin to meet Géronte. Scapin tells Géronte that Octavio's wife's family now want to have him killed because they think it is his fault that Argante wants the marriage annulled. Scapin offers to help Géronte escape the wife's family by hiding him in a sack. Once Géronte is in the sack Scapin pretends to be a member of the villainous family and interrogates himself over his master's whereabouts. He then pretends to be hit while protecting his master's father, whilst beating the sack and giving Géronte a good hiding! Eventually Géronte can take no more and gets out of the sack, Scapin runs away. Géronte is furious with Scapin's trick, but is met straightaway by Zerbinette. She is laughing at what has happened to her, and tells him the story: about how a young man fell in love with her, how the gypsies she was with would not part with her without being paid a large sum of money, and how the young man's foolish father was tricked out of a large sum of money by a servant. Géronte reveals that he is the father and leaves to search for his son. Zerbinette confesses to Sylvestre that she has 'spilt the beans'. Argante and Géronte meet together, realising that Scapin has hoodwinked them both. Géronte also bewails the news he has just received that his daughter from his secret first marriage, whom he has not seen for many years, has been lost at sea. At that moment his child's old nurse enters. She has been trying to seek out Géronte, unable to find him because he had changed his name. She confirms that Géronte's daughter is near at hand, but she also announces that his daughter is married – without his consent because they had not been able to find him. Argante and Géronte, surprised but happy, go to see Hyacinthe. Sylvestre brings Scapin up to date with events and warns him that the old men are after him. Octavio tells his father he will remain married to his wife whatever his father thinks, only to find that his father is more than happy with the match as his son has in fact made the desired match himself. Zerbinette apologises to Géronte for laughing at his predicament, but he still refuses to let her be married to his son. Léandre enters to declare that the gypsies have just revealed that she came from Naples and from a well-to-do family. He shows a bracelet which the gypsies also took – Argante recognises the bracelet and realises that Zerbinette is his own long-lost daughter! Carlo brings in Scapin, dying, mortally injured by a falling mason's hammer, and seeking forgiveness for his sins. Argante and Géronte forgive him everything and everyone goes in for the wedding feast.

Notice the plot structure. The play uses stock characters – masters and servants, rich fathers, lovers, lost children, scoundrels – in conventional story lines – the lost child is rediscovered, the thwarted lovers find true happiness, the wily servant outwits his master. This kind of narrative structure, which may to some modern audiences seem a little contrived and cliché-ridden, nonetheless has a long and healthy pedigree. The plot is based on the *Phormio* of the Roman playwright Terence, which Molière knew well, and also draws on the tricks and traditions of the Italian commedia dell'arte (a successful Italian troupe shared the Palais Royal with Molière's company). Scapin is the son of Brighella, a well established stock character within the commedia repertoire; he is a crafty character whose name comes from the Italian for 'escape' or 'run away'. Molière's intention in writing and presenting this play was thus two-fold: this play is an unashamed demonstration of his skill and wit as a playwright and an actor (Molière himself played Scapin); and, it is a clear acknowledgement of the importance and value of such traditional skills and knowledge, skills and knowledge that are part of the foundations on which he built his more ambitious and innovative plays. On another level there is some evidence that Molière produced *Scapin* for more strategic reasons – his company had struggled to compete with the commercial success of the Italian troupe in Paris, *Scapin* was an attempt to reclaim the popular ground on his own terms. No doubt Copeau too believed in the need to provide an introduction to his new and experimental staging ideas that was also popular and accessible.

WHY DID COPEAU CHOOSE THIS PLAY?

For Copeau, the decision to produce any play by Molière could never be accidental. Molière was a profound and lasting source of inspiration for him: an example of the role of playwright/director/actor/manager which he himself played within his company, a representative of the values which he was seeking to re-establish in French theatre. Copeau was later to pronounce that, 'It was under the invocation of Molière that the Vieux-Colombier was founded' (Copeau 1990: 142). Copeau's interest in Molière's short farces was motivated primarily by a wider interest in their roots in the lively and popular traditions of the commedia dell'arte rather than by any literary or academic interest.

Les Fourberies de Scapin is a playful piece of writing – it invites the actor to enjoy the act of performing, to use their skills with delight and to celebrate the theatricality of the stage. Copeau toyed with the idea that playwrights such as Molière and Shakespeare, who were not just writers but were actors as well, embedded into their writing indicators for the actor, subtle suggestions of movement, gesture, style, rhythm, character, and atmosphere: 'When a text is created for dramatic life, there is a necessary *mise en scène* within the work itself' (ibid.: 144). Though not completely wedded to the idea, he certainly found the notion of reading a text in this way an 'agreeable and fertile' (ibid.) approach for the actor. He thus understood the actor's job in relation to the task of discovering such indicators and translating them into action. It is in this sense that an actor can then be said to be 'obedient' to the text. Copeau suggests that such a reading of a theatrical text is not immediately evident to the literary critic, or to the academic, but that the ability to read a dramatic text as *theatre* is central to the staging of a text (and central to the skills of the actor). In order to read in this way, the actor requires an understanding of the playful possibilities of theatre – the actor must grasp how the internal logic of the *action* may be more important than any literal interpretation of what is spoken. Scapin's ruse to deceive Géronte into a painful beating, for instance, is pure theatre, illustrating how magical and fantastical the tricks of the performer can be. To the reader it seems little more than a clumsy piece of traditional stage business, hard to believe and lacking in psychological sophistication – but such a reading misses the point that Molière is trying to make. At one and the same time we see Scapin behave as a loyal servant protecting his master from a villain, and the old man getting kicked in the sack by the same servant – we see the actor playing a rogue playing a loyal servant. The logic of Scapin's actions and movements in this particular scene flow not from a simple psychological reading of the text, but from the logic of the body (what movement could follow from the position I am in now) and the logic of the imagination (how can I play with this situation or with this movement). Scapin's tricks are thus the tricks of the actor – we see both what is and what is not, we see the body transform and the imagination fly. The play is also a farce and relies upon pace, rhythm and timing to achieve its full comic effect, always balanced perilously on the edge of collapse and disaster. The actor playing Scapin must flirt with the possibility of failure, of being caught out by the master he is beating; the pretence must be played on a knife-edge of risk and believability. For Copeau, the particular features of farce, and of this play in particular, are not just comic devices but also represent the poetics of theatre *in action*, and indeed the fragility of our hold on life itself. The play provided a perfect arena in which Copeau could maximise the expressive effect of the rhythm and dynamics of the actor's movement. In fact, it is the play's very simplicity that makes it so attractive as a 'play-space' for the actor's imagination: 'There is in a work like *Les Fourberies de Scapin* a kind of playful elasticity which communicates, which allows the actor to be truly creative' (Copeau in Molière 1951: 28, author's translation).

STAGING

THE STAGE SPACE

For Copeau's first production of *Les Fourberies* in 1917 at the Garrick Theatre, New York, the existing stage space was transformed. The stage surround was stripped of its conventional decoration and left simple, grey and empty, with a small platform (*le tréteau*) placed centre-stage. The proscenium arch was opened up, allowing the stage space to connect more directly with the auditorium. Four years earlier Copeau had written that his rejuvenated theatre would require a bare stage (Copeau in Cole and Chinoy 1970) and now, finally, here it was. The bare stage and the raised platform were intended to emphasise the presence of the actor, bringing the audience's attention to their movement and footwork. The platform consisted of four large, square pieces of wood, raised on trestles. It was accessed by five staircases each with four steps, two of the staircases being at the front and one on each of the other three sides. Between the front two sets of steps were several cubes which acted as a bench. For Copeau, this meant that: 'The stage is already action, it gives material form to the action' (Copeau in Knapp 1988: 208). The audience saw only the bare stage, the platform, and, at the back of the stage, an orange velvet curtain. This was a controversial and innovative staging experiment to take to the heart of New York theatre. With only the simplest props and staging, the actors were required to use all their skills to summon up not only the illusion of character, but also of place, time and atmosphere. The production of *Les Fourberies de Scapin*, in this respect, provided a particular impetus for the company's early experiments with mime techniques. It challenged their abilities to create character, place, time and mood with the simplest of resources; no doubt giving those in the company such as Suzanne Bing, who were later to teach in the school, much food for thought.

The staging drew directly on Copeau's knowledge of the booth theatres of sixteenth century Europe. The raised platform, traditionally used to improve visibility for the audience, was the most direct reference to the earlier staging conventions. For the Vieux-Colombier company it created different levels for the stage action, a central focus for the audience's gaze, as well as a symbol of the simple authenticity they sought to bring to their playing. On a practical level, entrances and exits could no longer be as straightforward as opening or closing a door in a stage flat – the actor would need to enter several moments before their cue, in effect 'chasing' the action already on stage. The action would, in this manner, seem to 'wash' against the *tréteau* in waves, creating an ebb and flow of action and characters around the central focus point.

LIGHTING

Copeau had read about the ideas of Appia and Craig and had no doubt discussed ideas for lighting with both men during his meetings with them a few years earlier. In his early articles he had rejected the use of stage machinery:

> Being enthusiastic about the inventions of engineers or electricians always means giving usurped importance to canvas, painted cardboard, lighting arrangements – always means falling somehow or another into tricks. Old or new, we repudiate them all.
>
> (Copeau in Guicharnaud 1967: 301–2)

However, by the time he had completed his New York tour and returned to Paris, he had clearly recognised the value of a discreet, simple and unobtrusive use of lighting. His lighting plans for *Les Fourberies* drew on Craig's and Appia's innovations, and were also driven by his own determination to clear the stage space of unnecessary pretence. Michel Saint-Denis describes the stage of the 1920 revival as 'ruthlessly lit like a boxing ring' (Saint-Denis 1960: 22), implying that the lighting was bright, intense, and overhead – creating at once an image of openness and of focus, of risk and of excitement. The suggestion of a boxing ring, presumably enhanced by the presence of the raised platform of the *tréteau nu*, would have had some resonance for a cosmopolitan New York audience. The boxing ring had a special appeal within early twentieth century culture; boxing was a popular form of male physical education, and an equally popular spectator sport (Ruffini 1995). Copeau would have been aware of the associations he was drawing on and no doubt he was not averse to aligning his performers with the lithe nimble athleticism of the modern boxer.

For the new Paris season in 1920, Copeau and Jouvet installed a new lighting system which did away with the conventional footlights and made innovative use of new lighting technology. Jouvet designed and installed a set of revolving lanterns mounted at corners above the space, and also an array of lights concealed within a triangular box structure and suspended directly over the playing space. These overhead lights had the effect of flooding the stage with light, vividly illuminating the movement and actions of the actors and emphasising this above all else. The removal of footlights meant that the melodramatic effect of under-lighting the actors was avoided. The overhead lighting also helped to establish the heat and brilliance of the play's Neapolitan setting. Several years prior to Brecht's earliest work as a director, Copeau was already employing some of the staging techniques which the German playwright/director was to make part of his own, more overtly politicised, theatrical language (simple staging, bright lighting, acknowledgement of the audience's presence). Copeau's agenda was not political, and his work is not as well known, but he was no less influential in revolutionising lighting design for the modern stage.

THE ACTORS

The part of Scapin was played by Copeau. By the time of the first performance in New York, Copeau was thirty eight years old. He was taking on a major part in a classic farce, a part which required mobility, agility, comic timing and improvisatory skills which would challenge an actor half his age. Remarkably, given the other pressures on Copeau as leader of the company, he pulled it off with enormous success:

> Copeau brought out Scapin's turbulence, dynamism, and seemingly endlessly refreshing store of energy and imagination. He was movement incarnate, cascading motility, leaping here and there, with long and lithe strides, stopping but for seconds — just enough time to think up new tricks, new deceits, acrobatic stunts, and rogueries, thereby accomplishing his ends in the most theatrically perfect way possible.
>
> (Knapp 1988: 211)

Contemporary critics were struck by the plasticity of Copeau's performance, by 'its lightness of touch and mercurial swiftness of changing mood' (*Morning Sun*, 28 November 1917). The complete physicality of the performance contributed to the impression that every inch of the actor's body had become expressive: 'at once an athlete, a harlequin, a mimic and a comedian. He talks with his face, feet and hands as well as with his voice' (*Brooklyn Eagle*, 28 November 1917). At the same time, Copeau's understanding of rhythm and the dynamics of movement meant that his performance had 'smoothness' as well as 'dexterity and lithe vigour' (*The Literary Digest*, 15 December 1917). Acting the role of Scapin had a particular significance for Copeau, as he believed that Molière himself had played the part at the play's first performance. The connection between himself and his historical role model would not have been lost on him; like Molière, he was the creative and organisational linch-pin for his company. In this sense his performance can also be understood as a living homage to Molière, an interpretation further strengthened by his insertion of a company performance, after the New York opening, of a short devised spectacle 'The Crowning of Molière'.

Figure 3.1
Copeau in the role of Scapin in *Les Fourberies de Scapin* (1917). Scapin defends Argante

The part of Géronte was played by Louis Jouvet, one of Copeau's closest colleagues in the early days of the company. Jouvet was a bold actor, capable of giving full rein to the complete range of Géronte's emotions. He combined a humorous portrayal of physical decrepitude with a convincing display of Géronte's rapidly changing emotions of greed, fear, anger and shame. Several New York critics picked out Jouvet's performance as equally accomplished and equally important to the success of the production as that of Copeau. Remarkably, Jouvet's acting success was achieved alongside his many other significant responsibilities within the company, including supervising the redesign of the Garrick Theatre for the New York opening.

Both of these actors performed the same parts when the production was revived in Paris. The actress Jane Lory also continued in the part of Zerbinette. But the long and stressful New York tour had marked an important watershed for the company, revealing to Copeau those actors whom he could trust and with whom he could work in the future. Suzanne Bing, Robert Allard, Romain Bouquet, André Bacque and Georges Vitray — all of whom had previously performed in *La Nuit des Rois (Twelfth Night)* — joined the cast in Paris, no doubt bringing with them the rich experience of classical comedy they had gained from the earlier Shakespeare production. Copeau continued to devise short improvised prologues for the play, all of which drew on the traditions of the commedia dell'arte. His own direct involvement in the play gradually diminished until by the time of the open air performance in 1922 the part of Scapin was played by Georges Vitray.

REHEARSING AND ACTING: THE ACTOR'S APPROACH TO *LES FOURBERIES DE SCAPIN*

Though Copeau was probably aware of the kind of rigorous textual analysis which characterised Stanislavsky's System, this was not an approach which he felt was appropriate for the kind of theatre he was seeking to create. As Stanislavsky was eventually to realise himself, too much analysis can paralyse the actor's natural instincts for action and play:

> It isn't necessary to do analysis to get into a character or a play. It is an instinct or a talent which one either has or not, and this instinct alone gives the sense, the rhythm, the pulse of the character or of the play to the actor, just like a director.
>
> (Copeau in Molière 1951: 19, author's translation)

In rejecting heavy-handed text analysis Copeau was not promoting some form of anti-intellectualism, rather he was advocating a recognition of the importance of the actor's instinctual responses, without which no amount of analysis could make the part or the play live. For Copeau, a play is not simply a collection of characters, but rather a work of art which has its own particular physicality, emotionality, spatiality and dynamics. This meant that the actor needed to read the play thoroughly but sensitively in order to grasp its overall atmosphere, mood and emotional dynamics. He describes the process as similar to wood-carving – the latent shape and structure is revealed gradually and through the interplay of the actor's technique and artistic sensibility. As the rehearsal readings progress, it becomes clear what is working and what is not, what the actors are finding that is vital and living in the play. In this sense, Copeau's acting and rehearsal 'technique' is one of playful physical expression combined with introspection and intuitive under-standing. The actor and director have to bring into play their 'sense of theatre' – a sense which is a combination of critical understanding and of enjoyment and playfulness. Because this kind of understanding is not something which is easy to put into words, the emphasis in Copeau's rehearsals was on getting up and enacting the scenes, improvising and playing with the staging until it matched the director's and actors' senses of how the scene required itself to be played. Copeau allowed the actors to improvise around the text, sometimes for long periods, before draw-ing together elements from their play to form his final concepts for the *mise en scène* (Felner 1985: 42). The element that then linked the text and the movement in Copeau's technique was breath: 'To read a text, you must have sensitivity to the breath ... one speaks and acts as one breathes' (Copeau in Molière 1951: 24, author's translation).

This approach to acting and rehearsal was clearly well matched to a play such as *Les Fourberies de Scapin*. The play does not require deep and detailed analysis; its characters and its plot are easily recognisable and demand no profound psychological insights from the actors. The charac-ter's psychology, in so far as it is evident, is worn on the sleeve and exists less through subtext than through action and gesture. What is demanded is a sensitivity to rhythm and play, to the characters' physical pulse. Copeau believed that Molière's plays contained an implicit requirement for the actor to engage physically with the characters and the situations: 'There is a physical necessity made on the actor to be a dancer, feelingly to manifest this physical quality' (Copeau 1990: 144). The revealing word here is 'feelingly' – Copeau implies that the emotionality of the play is communicated not through the text or through the words, but through the physicality of the actor – their movements, gestures, actions. In so far as these physical elements are then organised, made meaningful and given intention, they become something approaching choreography. *Les Fourberies de Scapin* enabled Copeau to explore and develop this kind of approach to performance in detail. He realised that such a play could be interpreted as a kind of score for the actor – demonstrating to the young company how a writer could provide the sensitive actor with indications of the ebb and flow of the part and of the play, if they were open to receive it: 'This dance is in the text. It is not imagined' (ibid.). This kind of sensitive and sophisticated understanding of the dynamics of a play-text can easily be underestimated; several New York observers perceived nothing more than apparent exuberance, boisterousness and carelessness in the performances, with only the more perceptive critics recognising that these qualities were achieved with and through 'the most careful thought' (*New York Evening Post*, 28 November 1917).

PLAYING WITH OBJECTS

This vision of the rehearsal and acting process was an inclusive one, built on an holistic understanding of the actor's art. Thus, for Copeau even the smallest part of a scene has its value and importance. One wrong gesture or inflection can ruin the overall effect. Rather than ignore such problems Copeau preferred to go back on the scene and to modify the actions, checking how effectively everything hangs together. Rehearsing was a patient and careful procedure in which the company 'decoded' the play from words into actions whilst maintaining its essential coherence and quality. In a play such as *Les Fourberies de Scapin* even props had their special part to play and Copeau was insistent that their introduction into a scene had to be carefully worked out – on a bare stage props have an extra eloquence. We can look at an example of this by examining the way in which an umbrella or parasol was used to develop the playing of the character of Géronte. The parasol was itself an innovation – it is not specified in the original text, but was developed by Jouvet and Copeau as a simple way to indicate the heat of Naples and to provide the actor with a means of expression of character, intention and mood. The actor could open or close it, tap the ground, trail it behind him, point with it, use it as a weapon, or even as an extension of his own arm.

In pairs, look at the scene below (Act 3 Scene 2, author's translation) in which Scapin is talking to Géronte about the dangers facing him as a result of upsetting Octavio's bride's family.

GÉRONTE: What am I to do, my dear Scapin?
SCAPIN: I don't know, master – here's a bad business. I'm so scared for you I'm shaking from my head to my toes, and ... what was that!
GÉRONTE: Eh?
SCAPIN: No. No, no, it's nothing.
GÉRONTE: Can't you think of some way to get me out of this mess?
SCAPIN: I can think of one way; but I would run the risk of getting beaten myself.
GÉRONTE: Eh! Scapin, be a good servant: don't desert me, I beg you.
SCAPIN: I'll try my best. I have a soft spot for you which won't let me leave you defenceless.
GÉRONTE: You will be rewarded for it, I assure you. I promise you can have these clothes, when I've worn them a little longer.
SCAPIN: Wait. Here's an idea, and I think it just might save your skin. Get inside this sack.

Now, without the text, explore how both Géronte and Scapin might use the parasol:

- defending
- emphasising
- hiding
- dragging
- disguising
- protecting
- comforting
- restraining
- pushing away
- pointing/indicating
- offering
- getting attention
- avoiding/dodging

> Now build a sequence which works with the lines, trying to keep the playfulness which you had when improvising. Look carefully at how your sequence works and consider also its rhythmic shape and structure – when is it hectic, when nimble, when slow and when frenetic. To what extent does the parasol assist in this? How much does it become an extension of the actor's body? How does it help to clarify meaning and intention? Can it be transformed to serve any other purpose?

PLAYING STOCK CHARACTERS

The playing of stock characters is fraught with dangers, especially for the inexperienced or lazy actor. It can be only too easy to slip into a characterisation which is clichéd, two dimensional and predictable. Copeau recognised the challenge that a play like *Les Fourberies de Scapin* represented for his young troupe, but believed that the solution lay in trusting in Molière:

> Molière never created a mundane character, a stock character, as we say, or a fill-in, because he was a man of the theatre and he wrote for actors.
>
> (Copeau 1990: 144)

The characters may initially seem simple and stereo typical, but this is a misapprehension born from the expectation of psychological and social realism, from the dead-weight of tradition, and from a misunderstanding of the nature of this kind of comedy. Copeau saw this play as 'pure' theatre, and by this he meant that the internal logic which bound the play together and gave it coherence was not psychological, political or even entirely narrative, but essentially theatrical. Its driving energy was not that of the gentle drawing room comedy, but the lively 'ferocious' all-consuming energy of the commedia dell'arte. To play such characters demands a complete physical, vocal and mental commitment, as well as enormous fitness, agility and control on the part of the actors. The characters need to be able to turn on a sixpence, constantly on their toes in order to survive the twists and turns that fate throws at them. To achieve this kind of playing, actors need to be performing 'in the moment' – alive to all that is going on around them, to the possibilities their role offers, and to the potential offered by the objects, spaces and actors around them.

PLAYING THE RHYTHM

Copeau came to theatre via the written media of playwriting and journalism, yet very early on in his career as a theatre director he realised the importance of the physical aspects of performance. We have already examined his commitment to the physical training of the actor – for the kind of theatre that he wanted to make he needed actors who were fit, strong, flexible and agile. Such physical ability needed however to be shaped and directed through the operation of a guiding set of aesthetic principles in order that it might become truly integral to the actor's art. The answer for Copeau, as for several other early twentieth century theatre practitioners, came from the analysis of rhythm. Copeau, like Stanislavsky, Appia and Meyerhold, knew of the work of Emile Jaques-Dalcroze, and would have had some knowledge of the movement theories of Etienne Marey, Georges Demeny and Paul Souriau. Although by 1920 Copeau had rejected Jaques-Dalcroze's work as too formulaic and reductive, and Eurhythmics had been replaced by Hébertisme in the School curriculum, yet this should not be taken to mean that Copeau's interest in rhythm and acting was in any sense diminished. Rhythmic movement was, for Copeau, a way of opening up the actor to the rhythm of a piece of spoken text. He saw a direct relationship between reading dramatic text and rhythmic movement training (Copeau 1990: 58), which led him to believe that this kind of training must form the basis for a holistic training regime for the new actor. Copeau was critical of Jaques-Dalcroze's work with movement and spoken text, he found it affected and even a little ridiculous; but he knew instinctively that rhythmic awareness was a skill which the actor could and should possess.

What Copeau sought was to incorporate and internalise the sense of rhythm, in much the same way as Stanislavsky encouraged his students to explore what he called 'the inner tempo-rhythm' of a part. When he came to work on a play such as *Les Fourberies de Scapin*, Copeau saw immediately the importance of rhythm to the acting and to his own *mise-en-scène*. Right from the start of the play, Copeau wanted the actors' movements to give dramatic expression to the rhythms and dynamics within the play. Let's look at the opening scene and at Copeau's notes:

The dialogue above appears quite bald and functional; Molière is using the scene simply to establish the plot and the characters. The structure is that of a double act routine, a rapid question-and-answer exchange between the anxious lover/son and the shifty servant. Let's look at what Copeau does with this section of the scene. According to Copeau's notes and stage directions (Molière 1951: 33), Octavio should enter suddenly from the left, extremely agitated, arms gesturing wildly to the sky, and pacing from left to right at the front of the stage. As Octavio gets to centre-stage Silvestre appears, on the same path across the stage, moving very slowly in contrast to his young master. As he does so he eats sunflower seeds which he takes from the pocket of his jacket. Octavio rounds on Silvestre, who responds incoherently, still chewing. This interplay continues between them, varying and developing as Octavio becomes more and more urgent and exasperated – pulling on his hat, waving his hands and so on. The exchange ends with Octavio walking backwards in front of Silvestre who slowly gains ground, finally reaching the steps on the right where he sits.

Straight away we can see that Copeau wants the two characters to be clearly differentiated by the rhythm of their movement. Furthermore, he intends that the rhythm of the movement creates and embodies the dramatic impact of the scene. In this scene, the rhythmic interplay comes from the rapid, anxious pacing of Octavio and the slow matter-of-fact chewing of Silvestre. Despite Octavio's role as the master and despite his attempts to impose his urgent rhythm on his servant, we can tell that it is Silvestre who is setting the pace and controlling the game. He plays with his master's agitation, setting a dramatic counter-context for the driving love story. Elsewhere in the play, the staging itself actively draws attention to the actor's rhythm. Copeau realised that the sound of footsteps, leaps, falls and the tapping of sticks and umbrellas could all variously function to announce someone's arrival, draw the audience's or the actor's attention, build suspense, increase the noise of a scene, or punctuate speech. Michel Saint-Denis (1982: 29) describes how the platform stage 'intensified, in a pleasant manner, the sounds made on it, either by the stamping, jumping feet of the younger characters or by the slow stomping of their elders accompanied by the tapping of their walking sticks.' John Rudlin (1986: 81) picks up on Saint-Denis' memories of the 'by-play of sound' created as the actors leapt from 'the hard coldness of the cement floor up to the warm, resounding wooden platform' (Saint-Denis 1982: 29), pointing out the manner in which the sounds created by Scapin's feet and Géronte's movements help to bring the comedy of the 'sack scene' in Act 3 Scene 2 to a riotous and noisy climax. We can see a similar but different effect later in the same scene when Géronte dances with rage as he listens to Zerbinette's story of his own foolishness – providing a counterpoint to the rhythm of her bubbling laughter. Similarly at the beginning of Act 2 Scene 1, we see Argante, hat in hand and dripping with sweat, bustle along in what may have seemed something like an agitated dance, performing what Knapp describes as 'arabesques' (Knapp 1988: 211) around the platform. In contrast, Géronte walks with short steps, sheltering his head from the sun with his parasol. The contrast is physical; there is an auditory and a visual contrast between the two old men, producing a counterpoint of rhythms and postures.

With a partner, walk around the room, establishing a shared rhythm to your walk. Your walk should be neither too fast nor too slow. Now, while one of you maintains that rhythm, the other tries to walk at half the rhythm, and then twice the rhythm. Finally try to walk at the counter-tempo, in between your partner's footfalls. Change over. To finish, improvise an argument with your partner as you walk, allowing the changes in rhythm to take place as you engage with the argument with your partner. Perhaps you slow down your rhythm to make a point, or speed up your rhythm to express your frustration. Try to play with the rhythm, rather than let it dominate.

Now pick a scene from the play – an argument, a love scene, a disagreement, or a plotting scene – and explore how the rhythm of the two characters' walks (or gestures, or speech) could be used to express physically the nature of the interplay between them. This same exercise could be developed further by using sticks, parasols, sacks, bags of money, food or a number of other properties as the medium for the rhythmic interplay.

PLAYING THE SPACE

Copeau intended the *tréteau* to be central to the staging of the play. In order to achieve this, he had to explore how the platform could be used as an integral part of the drama. Copeau discovered that as well as providing a clear and open space on which to expose the rhythmic interplay of the characters' movements, the platform stage could also function to create a physical expression of the characters' age and status – revealing their particular physical abilities. Copeau described it as operating, in this play, as a 'trap for old men' – giving them a sense of peril and danger and of the unknown. The young characters could leap on and off the platform, sometimes even using it as a kind of spring-board. The older characters were forced to clamber on and off, teeter on the steps or even go round it like an obstacle. The platform represented the status of the characters – achieving the platform indicating that a character had managed to assume status and/or authority within a scene – and of course the platform was dominated for most of the scenes by the figure of Scapin! How different this kind of playing is from the naturalistic drama – space is used symbolically, acoustically, rhythmically and dynamically, it comes alive and is an expressive element within the theatre event. The actors' posture, movements and gestures, and the fluid images which Copeau's *mise en scène* generate, are all shown in vivid relief against the bare stage and the *tréteau*. The effect is both sculptural and musical, creating dynamic living images and rhythmic counterpoints between characters. Even simple movements and gestures function musically, accumulating energy and rhythm, building their effect on the audience's imagination.

With no complex set changes to perform, the scenes can flow smoothly, quickly and efficiently one into the next – sometimes to magical effect, sometimes providing deliciously poignant overlaps as one character exiting nearly meets another entering. Place is established by a word and a gesture – in fact the overlay of fictive space (Naples) and theatrical space (the Vieux-Colombier stage) is made explicit through the very simplicity of the setting. This calls for a style of acting which is equally direct, and which can also move smoothly between the fictive and the overtly theatrical. Copeau found this quality in the naïve play of children and it is this playful but absorbed energy which seems to permeate his production notes.

Copeau's staging ideas have influenced several of the major figures of contemporary theatre. Peter Brook used similarly simple devices in several of his productions and theatrical experiments over the last thirty years. For his journey across Africa in the early 1970s his company used a large carpet to delineate the playing space; for his production of *La Tempête* he used a circular pit of sand; and, for his production of *Ubu*, a large industrial cable drum. Just as Copeau had done before him, Brook consciously made use of the qualities and associations of the materials and shapes of the set structures for his productions. The simple designs helped to establish the rhythms and dynamics of the piece as a whole. Both Brook and Copeau clearly searched for the simplest form of staging that would still be able to create a world which the play/text/improvisations could meaningfully inhabit. It is also possible to see similarities with the work of Steven Berkoff, who is equally sensitive to the playful possibilities of movement and space, using direction, rhythm and movement dynamics within bare spaces to establish place, mood and a sense of theatrical poetry.

A DIFFERENT KIND OF REALISM

Copeau was aware of Stanislavsky's production of *Les Fourberies de Scapin* at the Moscow Art Theatre. He had already noted that, 'Stanislavsky's *mise en scène* is unnecessarily realistic. In order to explain Scapin's sack, Stanislavsky puts a boat loaded with grain sacks at the back of the set, from which Scapin borrows the prop in the sack scene' (Copeau 1990: 261). For Copeau the 'location' of the sack was not important, it was there because it was needed: 'The sack was a traditional accessory in the theatre of the sixteenth century. It was frequently used' (Copeau in Molière 1951: 28, author's translation). Likewise, when the sack was finished with Géronte can simply kick it into the wings. Stanislavsky's productions relied for their veracity and inner logic on carefully worked out naturalistic details; Copeau believed that this kind of realism ignored the theatricality at the heart of Molière's theatre. Whereas Stanislavsky's approach to acting might certainly be capable of being adapted to non-naturalistic plays, he seems to have struggled to develop an approach to staging which was as flexible. Copeau wrote in his notes that to base classical productions on the principles of realism was tantamount to a betrayal – it went against everything those plays stood for (ibid.: 19). This is of course not to say that Copeau entirely rejected realism – he advocated the use of elements of realism in order to maintain an appropriate feeling of vitality and relevance within the production – but he did not feel bound by the aesthetic logic of realism, and would transpose anachronistic realistic elements into period situations because he felt it was justified within the inner dynamics of the play (e.g. Géronte's umbrella). He rejected whole-heartedly the declamatory vocal delivery of the Comédie-Française, preferring instead a delivery which was natural, fluid and sensitive to the events on stage. Copeau specialised in giving dramatic readings – something he continued to do for most of his working life – and the simple, direct style of the reading was a style which infused the vocal delivery of the whole company. If this occasionally led to a slightly austere and presentational vocal style, nonetheless in the right circumstances it allowed the words to 'work' on the listener rather than requiring the actor to 'emote'.

SYMBOLISM AND SCAPIN

Instead of a laboured realism, Copeau chose a simple bare staging – a choice which was undoubtedly influenced by his memories of the work of Craig and Appia. A clear stage would make room for the flow of movement which would bring the rhythms and dynamics of the play alive. Perhaps Copeau wanted, like Craig, to move beyond the suggestion of time and place towards some timeless representation of mood, ideas and a deeper dramatic reality, but he preferred to work on a less monumental and abstract scale. His staging did not set out to dwarf the actors but to provide them with a space which let their actions live and breath, and which allowed the audience to feel closer to the stage and less intimidated by it. Like Craig he had a fine eye for the flow of lines of movement and action, but whereas Craig seemed happier working with inanimate objects, Copeau preferred the living movement of his actors. For both the aim seems to have been to create a space that in effect generates movement rather than simply framing it.

> Two years ago, I put on *Les Fourberies de Scapin*. In order to revive the movement with which the play was presented, I thought it advisable to conceive a stage lay-out which forcibly produced movement. So I imagined the tréteau, surrounded on four sides by steps, built in the centre of the stage, in order to compel the actors constantly to change position.
>
> (Copeau 1990: 145)

Copeau did not think of his theatre as 'symbolist', however he was aware of the symbolist movement and was in some respects closer to symbolism in his staging than to realism. His approach to staging aimed to humanise symbolism, bringing the scale of the poet's inner vision down to a more personal size. The characters of his dramas were always more than ciphers for the poet's inner mind – though Copeau championed the playwright as the poet of the theatre, he would never conceive of a theatre in which the actor/character was a mere pawn to the playwright's vision.

A useful comparison can be made with the early work of the London-based physical theatre company Théâtre de Complicité, for example *A Minute Too Late* (1984) or *Anything For A Quiet Life* (1987). In these shows, a seemingly simple and essentially comic narrative is set up around a group of clearly delineated characters; at the same time, a minimal but flexible staging allows the actors to pursue wonderful flights of fantasy and imagination, executed with physical skill and acrobatic agility. The whirling plot narratives, and the dreamlike fantasies weaved around them, leave us touchingly aware of the fickleness of fate and the futility of our struggle to stay on top of events. The lightness, joy, freshness and technical expertise of these productions gives us some insight into the possible effect which a production such as *Les Fourberies de Scapin* might have achieved, as well as demonstrating the continuing influence of Copeau's innovations.

FRAMING THE EVENT

For the first performance Copeau decided that the production needed some kind of introduction. In fact the evening was advertised as being composed of three parts: *L'Impromptu du Vieux-Colombier* by Jacques Copeau, *Les Fourberies de Scapin* by Molière, and *Le Couronnement de Molière (The Crowning of Molière)*. There were several reasons for this. On one level Copeau was simply copying a tradition used by many renaissance playwrights – the use of a prologue and epilogue served to introduce the company and the work to an audience. In the context of the New York tour, the framing pieces also served to provide an introduction to the style of the company and to create an ambience for the evening as a whole. *L'Impromptu* offered the audience a form of introduction to the actors, using a format which was both traditional and yet which also emphasised the theatricality of the event. After a welcome address by Suzanne Bing, Copeau called on the 'spirit' of the theatre, represented by the dancer Jessmin Howarth, to inspire the company. His words echo Oberon's instructions to Puck, invoking the mystery of theatre tradition and the ritual power and magic of the stage. *L'Impromptu* finishes with Copeau calling out to the company who respond in chorus that they are ready, the stage manager then gives the traditional signal for the start of the play by knocking three times and the play begins and is acted 'sans interruption dans un mouvement rapide' (Copeau 1984: 175). The lack of an interval and the rapid pace clearly signal Copeau's conviction that the artistic integrity of the production was more important than the need to accommodate the conventional breaks. He was certainly convinced enough of the benefits of a form of improvised prologue to invent several other semi-improvised scenarios to introduce *Les Fourberies de Scapin* when it was revived again in Paris.

At the end of the play, after the curtain calls, Copeau placed the other short piece, *Le Couronnement de Molière*. A bust of Molière was brought on to the middle of the *tréteau*, and placed on a pedestal. The bust then became the focal point of a solo dance-drama; a performance quite probably choreographed by Jessmin Howarth, and thus drawing on a mixture of Ancient Greek and Eurhythmic references. After this homage in movement, the dancer lifts a flute to his mouth and produces a sound which is echoed by the chorus of actors in the wings. The ritual and symbolic nature of the piece is reinforced by the appearance of several figures – Aristophanes, Terence, Plautus, Harlequin, Shakespeare, and others – representing the comic traditions of Europe – who also dance in homage to Molière. Eventually all the various symbolic figures dance a *farandole* around the stage. The music ends, and Jessmin Howarth enters as the spirit of the Vieux-Colombier. She dances, finishing by introducing on to the stage Copeau's two small children, Marie-Hélène and Edi, each holding a dove in a cage (a symbol of the Vieux-Colombier Theatre) which they offer to the bust of Molière. Copeau enters in the costume of Scapin, under the robe he wore for *L'Impromptu*. He holds the hand of his young son, Pascal, who carries a crown of laurels. They approach the bust; Copeau recites a homage to Molière, at the end of which he lifts up his son who crowns the bust with the laurels.

The ritual elements of *Le Couronnement de Molière* are clearly intentional. Copeau meant this final part of the evening as a serious and artistic act of homage. As with *Les Fourberies de Scapin* it is easy to see that in the wrong hands this piece could seem trite, quaint, and overly reverential. It is rescued by the qualities which mark out so much of Copeau's best work: its simplicity, its bravery, its sincerity, its purposeful integration of dance, voice and movement, and its ability to bring into play the 'heart' of the company – its beliefs, its family ethos and its theatrical reference points. There is an element of the self-conscious about the framing of the main performance in this way. Copeau spent a lifetime as an educator – teaching, lecturing and giving demonstrations – and an element of the educational and expository lingers around the manner in which the opening night was presented. But before being too quickly critical of Copeau, we must recognise that the impulse behind the whole event was not that the audience should forget themselves, but that they should be awakened to the extraordinary power and poetry of theatre and its particular relationship with its audience and with western cultural history. It is all too easy to view *L'Impromptu* and *Le Couronnement de Molière* as slightly embarrassing indulgences on the part of Copeau, but this is to miss their significance as important and carefully crafted framing devices for the main play, and to ignore the importance of these apparent dramatic 'trinkets' as foretastes of the more sophisticated and complex work, seven years later, of Les Copiaus.

CRITICAL REACTION

The reaction of the critics to *Les Fourberies de Scapin* also reveals something of the significance of this production. Some American critics found it difficult to accept a theatre production which was so radically different from the theatre traditions they were used to, but many could appreciate the innovatory value of the enterprise. The deceptive simplicity of Copeau's production meant that there was little to say about the décor and design. Some critics found it difficult to see why Copeau had chosen a light farce as his opening production – surely notable European theatre must be sombre and portentous, not playful and frivolous.

> The grand qualities of the play were lost on the American critics, surfeited as they were by the harsh and glittering obviousness of American theatre. The pure spirit of comedy, playing upon passions and foibles of simple human beings, could not hold them; it seemed not only superficial, but unsophisticated – surprising, coming from the French.
>
> (Knapp 1988: 212)

Despite some puzzlement over the opening 'Impromptu' and the final 'Crowning', there was general recognition of the quality of the performances: 'the performance of Molière's boisterous and primitive farce was accomplished in excellent style ... there was always celerity, vigor, vivacity and veracity in the performance' (*Morning World*, 28 November 1917). It is evident that the company impressed the New York audience's with their skilful ensemble playing, perhaps more so because of the lack of décor and the simplicity of the play. Though the minimalist staging qualities of the production confused some critics, others recognised the possibilities the staging offered for the 'lively actor, childlike in his playful eagerness' (*Boston Transcript*, 28 November 1917). John Corbin, writing in the *New York Sunday Times* (December 1917) also recognised the innovatory success of the *tréteau nu*: 'an artistic perception as subtly intelligent as it is original'. The irreverent informality of the event clearly disturbed some, one letter to the *New York Times* (5 December 1917) complained that Copeau's 'conception of the character [of Scapin], his blending of the clown and of Mephistopheles makes a bizarre combination' and considered the whole production grotesque, annoying and bewildering. Others found the simple staging over-strained, 'to the point where it actually interposes a barrier to imagination instead of encouraging imagination' (George Nathan, *Chicago Herald*, 16 December 1917). But, in general, all relished the vitality of the performances:

> Their manner was so fresh and impulsive that the spectator could not escape the conviction that much of the business was actually improvised ... beyond all else one noted the physical freedom and poise of the players, who had been trained not as actors alone, but as happy vigorous animals.
>
> (*Boston Transcript*, 28 November 1917)

Copeau himself had been a critic. He understood the importance of critical reviews – for the financial success of the company, and for the success of its artistic mission. The Copeau Archives in the Bibliothèque nationale de France contain an extensive set of reviews from both the New York and Paris productions. They confirm that many of Copeau's aims were successfully achieved. Furthermore, they help us to understand something of the significance of the production: the new standards it set for vigorous and spontaneous ensemble playing; the innovations it made in staging methods and lighting; and, the energy and rhythmic musicality of the physically trained performer.

WHERE NEXT: A NEW COMMEDIA?

Copeau revived this production several times, culminating in the open-air performance in the Place Saint-Sulpice in 1922, and we can assume that he did so at least in part because it was good box office and popular with his audience and supporters. However, throughout his career Copeau refused to be driven solely by financial imperatives, and he would not have returned repeatedly to *Les Fourberies de Scapin* if it did not also embody the essential features of the theatre towards which he aspired. *Les Fourberies de Scapin* provided Copeau with the opportunity to develop his ideas about popular theatre, the physical actor, the ensemble and the *tréteau nu* by testing them in the public arena. The production needs to be seen as complementary to his work in the Vieux-Colombier School, and as part of the journey towards his later work with Les Copiaus. Key features of this production were to reappear in the work in

Figure 3.2
Les Fourberies de Scapin in performance in the Place Saint-Sulpice, Paris (May 1922), with Georges Vitray as Scapin and Suzanne Bing (second from right) as Hyacinthe

Burgundy: the open and simple staging, the direct physical playing, the rapport between stage and audience, the use of simple texts and the emphasis on the theatrical event. In many senses then, we can see the seeds of Copeau's later work more clearly in *Les Fourberies de Scapin* than in many other productions.

4

ACROBATS OF THE SOUL: PRACTICAL EXERCISES FOR THE ACTOR

Talk to any student actor at an established drama school and they will tell you about the animal studies they have been doing, the neutral mask work which underpins their movement work, the group and ensemble exercises they do, and perhaps the classes they have had on commedia dell'arte or clowning. These exercises are the backbone of contemporary actor training, deeply informing much of the student actor's development, shaping and building their psycho-physical technique. The exercises that follow give the reader an opportunity to experience (or, if they prefer, to review) the extent to which Copeau's ideas have become part of the international language of occidental actor training.

EDUCATING THE ACTOR: THE CONTEXT

One of the fundamental principles underpinning the training at the Vieux-Colombier School, and at Pernand-Vergelesses for Les Copiaus, was the education of the actor's senses through observation, action and imitation. This was the base on which all subsequent development must take place, for Copeau believed that the art and skill of the actor lay in their ability to be sensitive and responsive to the emotional resonances set off by actions. Since the days of Roman oratory, actors have understood that there is a particular relationship between physical actions, movements and gestures, and the expression or communication of feelings, emotions, thoughts and ideas. Various attempts were made during the nineteenth century to codify such relationships by seeking to align specific emotional states with specific gestures and actions – for instance, Charles Darwin's work on *The Expression of the Emotions in Man and Animals* (1872) and **François Delsarte**'s taxonomy of gestures and their expressive significance (see Taylor 1999).

François Delsarte (1811–1871) was an influential movement teacher, based in Paris during the mid-nineteenth century. His original career as a singer was curtailed as a result of poor voice teaching and over-use. His course in 'Applied Aesthetics' included a codification of physical and vocal expression, based on his observation of natural behaviour, and informed by his strong religious beliefs. His pupil Steele MacKaye took his teachings to America where they met with considerable success and popularity.

Copeau's training regime, while it clearly owes something to this intellectual heritage, sought to discover an approach that was more organic. The scientific analysis of emotion was of no use to the actor, whose requirement was more urgent – how could the actor generate a seemingly spontaneous, truthful and sincere response to fictional and rehearsed events. The actor needs the sensitivity to recognise, identify and focus on their responses to the world around them, and the flexibility, fitness and poise to be able to do so spontaneously, truthfully and without 'contamination'. To do all this, the student actor needed a training which would prepare them to be agile, aware, and alert. The work was of necessity physical, building on notions of 'force and duration, place, orientation, balance, lightness, heaviness, gentleness, elasticity, resistance, direction' (Bing in Kusler 1979: 21), notions closely related to the work of Jaques-Dalcroze and **Rudolf Laban**.

Copeau's exercises can look deceptively simple; perhaps even old-fashioned and over-familiar. They are actually very challenging in their simplicity, taking the actor to the heart of their craft and demanding a subtle form of what John Rudlin calls 'practical intelligence' (1986: xv). Copeau did not share some of his European contemporaries' fascination for the mechanical or scientific; he turned to nature for his models rather

Rudolf Laban (1879–1958) began his career as an artist, before establishing a successful and influential career in Germany as a choreographer and dance analyst. In 1939 he fled from Nazi Germany to England, where he spent the rest of his life. His analysis of movement in relation to its dynamic qualities of time, space and direction has been influential in the development of educational dance, movement therapy and movement training for actors.

than to modern paradigms. In this sense, it is important to recognise Copeau's intention that the exercises he proposed should be employed as more than a set of techniques or tricks. Copeau's mission was to develop the 'actor-artist', a creative and mature individual whose best work grew within a group of fellow actors. Such a vision was directly antithetical to the conventional system of the time, whereby a student went to a dramatic academy, got an acting job, and then never thought again about their skills and techniques. Such a system favoured the cynically ambitious, the lazy but talented, and the well-connected. If Copeau's exercises still have currency now, it is because the same challenges, and the same complacencies, still exist.

Many of Copeau's exercises have become commonplace in drama teaching and training over the last fifty years. However, although Copeau discusses some of his exercises in several of his texts (including outlines of training schemes for the Vieux-Colombier School), nowhere does he list or describe all his exercises in precise detail in the manner of Stanislavsky or Michael Chekhov. This creates a situation where Copeau's teaching practice is better preserved through its dissemination in the classroom than it is through the written word. We can however start to create some maps for those seeking to explore this territory by piecing together the details of some important exercises from evidence in his texts, and from the writings of some of his students, actors and colleagues. In attempting to make the exercises useful and relevant to a twenty-first century readership it has inevitably been necessary in places to fill out and develop the original directions and descriptions. Where I have done so I have tried to ensure that additions are in the spirit of Copeau's work and aims. In doing this I have drawn on my own experiences at the École Jacques Lecoq in Paris, a system of training which owes a significant debt to Copeau's legacy. A structured sequence of exercises is proposed, offering students an opportunity to engage with aspects of the experiential and creative journey which Copeau provided for the student actor. The exercises are presented in the spirit of Copeau's work – not as a description of what Copeau's actors did, but as a list of instructions for the interested practitioner. The exercises I have chosen fall into the four broad categories that mark out Copeau's most significant contributions to the development of actor training.

1   *Physical preparation* This section looks at appropriate preparation for the exercises which follow. Suggestions are made for the kinds of exercises which might successfully build awareness, precision and expressive skills, and which could organically lead into exercises in improvisation.

2   *Improvisation* The use of improvisation as a focussed technique for the training of actors or for the creation of a coherent dramatic performance was an innovative practice at this time. The exercises suggested by Copeau challenge the actor to respond in simple, direct and expressive ways to fundamental dramatic 'events' and stimuli.

3   *Mask-work* Mask-work further develops the expressive skills of the actor. Drawing on the abilities developed through the improvisation work, masks help the actor to develop clarity, to eliminate excess gesture and to expand the ability to portray character.

4   *Chorus* The final challenge for the performer is to place their own skills within the context of group creation. These exercises move the student further towards ensemble performance, and bring together all of the skills and knowledges developed in the earlier work.

BEFORE BEGINNING

ATTITUDE

Any performance training relies not just on a readiness of the body, but also on the creation of an appropriate attitude to work. Despite his artistic austerity and his commitment to the moral value of his art, Copeau encouraged his students and actors to work with a lightness and playfulness which is not frivolous, but which represents an openness to the imaginative potential of any exercise or scene. As you explore the exercises which follow do not take them too seriously, or too lightly – find a state of mind where you can allow your imagination to give life to your work, this will take time and may need long practice. Stay focused on each exercise until it is finished, and pay attention to the detail of each exercise. It may be useful to make notes of your experiences for later reflection and analysis.

AWARENESS

This lively imaginative engagement should extend to your relationship with fellow performers – be sensitive towards those you are working with. The simplest exercises often require us to reveal the most about ourselves; this is not possible without trust. Be ready to explore the potential that working together and in sensitive collaboration with the ideas, rhythms, dynamics and energies of others can bring. Do not allow sensitivity to others to become a lazy mirroring of their actions – try instead to develop a lively and playful awareness of the presence of others. Remain open to the effects of shared rhythm, shared space and shared emotion.

ENVIRONMENT

Make sure that you choose a warm and well lit space to work in, preferably big enough to allow for your group to move easily and safely around each other without danger of collisions. Wear neutral clothes that allow for free and comfortable movement. It is of course important that you can work without interruption or disturbance. It will be useful to have access to some gymnastic mats for tumbling work, and, if possible, some masks (neutral masks and commedia dell'arte character masks in particular) or mask-making facilities.

PHYSICAL PREPARATION

Every student actor faces the same problems at the start of every class. How should you prepare your body for work? What kind of preparation helps rather than hinders the work that will follow? Let us examine some of the approaches used by Copeau.

WARM-UP

A simple routine which includes stretching, relaxing and invigorating all the major muscle groups should be adequate – examples of suitable exercises can be found in various texts (e.g. Callery 2001). Ensure that you raise your heart-beat and increase your breathing rate for a sustained period within the warm-up routine – your breath and your pulse are the core of any preparation of the body for action. You can work from the list below:

- Swinging – arms, legs, torso – from side to side. Allow gravity to assist the movement.
- Stretching – reach up through the spine, out through the arms and through the legs in all directions. Explore the space around you.
- Rolling – down through the spine, gently allowing the spine to articulate and flex. Avoid tensing other muscles in the neck and shoulders at the same time.
- Run – on the spot. Then freeze and hold your position before starting again. Concentrate on energy, control, and balance.

ACROBATICS

For Copeau, acrobatics both demanded and developed physical freedom, rigorous articulation and precision, and better timing, in the student's work. Acrobatic work should only be undertaken after a good physical warm-up, and in a warm space with suitable equipment – mats, and assistants or 'spotters' (if necessary). Identify some basic acrobatic routines (for example forward rolls, backward rolls, handstands, cartwheels) with which you feel comfortable, and repeat them, bearing in mind the following:

- Control – where is each limb during the routine? Are all your energies focussed towards the purpose they have to achieve? Maintain a composed and balanced posture at the start and at the end of the routine.
- Co-ordination – how is your body working together as a whole? The whole of your body must be engaged in the action. Keep the body flexible and supple, but with muscular tone and good alignment.

- Centring – notice how the movements all move in and out from the centre of gravity, how energy is gathered and dispersed.
- Confidence – how does successful completion of the routine feel? The development of physical confidence is important for your stage presence. Decisiveness is important and not one movement should be accidental or unplanned.
- Notice the rhythm of the routine(s), the necessary pause between each movement. Gymnastics makes evident what Copeau calls 'muscular time' – the time required for the body to recover and prepare, for the body to re-centre before the energies move outwards again. Copeau observed this same kind of rhythmic poise in the work of clowns and comic dancers (Copeau 1990: 35). He used the image of a bird on a lawn to communicate the sense of alert, poised energy he was looking for – the controlled, focused action, followed by the balanced recovery. Can you identify this quality?
- You might also attempt some partnered work, such as balances where you stand on another's thighs, or simple vaults, such as leapfrog jumps. It is not advisable to attempt hand-springs, walk-overs or somersaults unless you are already proficient in gymnastics or have assistance from a trained coach.

ISOLATIONS

According to Barbara Kusler, exercises in 'the isolation of different parts of the body in movement' (1979: 21) were explored by Suzanne Bing as preparation for the physical expression of emotion and the presentation of character. Isolation of body parts in movement reinforces the control and co-ordination developed by the gymnastic work, placing it in a different context. Work your way through the following sequence:

- Start from a balanced, upright standing position.
- Shake out all over, releasing unnecessary tensions from your body, especially shoulders, neck, and chest.
- Start from the feet. Keeping the rest of the body as still as possible, raise one foot and explore the possibilities for movement available to it – rotation (turning on a central axis), translation (moving to one side), and inclination (bending off its central axis).
- Combine these options so that the relevant body part circles and flexes to explore all the space available to it. Work your way up the

body – feet, knees, legs, hips, torso, arms, wrists, fingers, neck/head – until the whole body has been fully articulated.

- Throughout, try to focus on moving only the particular body part or parts on which you have chosen to work.
- When you have finished, find a partner. With your partner, begin a silent dialogue using only one part of the body as your means of communication – head, shoulder, chest, hips, knees, elbows. Try not to mime your intentions, let your focus be on expressing your emotions through limited movement possibilities. Allow the 'dialogue' between you to develop its own logic, its own dynamics.
- Try using the same body parts, then try using different parts – what differences did you notice?
- Isolating one part of the body can be done by moving it when the rest of the body is still or by keeping it still while the rest of the body moves. Try some of the exercises above reversing the areas of movement and immobility. What is the effect?

These exercises were the basis on which Bing built her early exercises in mime; work which was to inspire Etienne Decroux's development of corporeal mime in the 1930s. Isolation gives focus to a particular body part, orientating other movements around it. In this manner it is possible to use isolation, as Kusler indicates above, as the starting point for the development of character. You can now explore this yourself as follows:

- Pick one body part and explore its movement in isolation.
- Now focus on isolated movements which are drawn from the movement vocabulary of 'everyday life' – fidgeting, watching, waiting, attracting attention, indicating.
- Allow the rest of the body to move as naturally as possible in the pursuit of simple aims – walking across the room, going to greet someone, avoiding other people, looking for something or someone. But allow the movement to begin from the isolated part and to be focused around that part. What might it mean to be a 'head' person, or a 'chest' person, or a 'right shoulder' person?
- What happens if instead of the movement being led by a particular body part, it is resisted by that part? What if the head, chest or right shoulder is withdrawn, the last body part to move?
- How do we read character out of posture in this way? How is the expression of emotion shaped by the body and its co-ordination?

- What effects do the speed of motion and the rate of transition into and from immobility have? If you move slowly or quickly into or out of immobility how does this effect dramatic impact and emotional resonance?

IMPROVISATION

> Improvisation is an art that has to be learned ... The art of improvising is not just a gift. It is acquired and perfected by study.
>
> (Copeau in Rudlin 1986: 44)

Whereas for Stanislavsky improvisation was a tool which helped to improve the rehearsal process, Copeau came to perceive the purpose of improvisation as much more profound. For Copeau, improvisation allowed his students 'to discover for themselves, within themselves, what acting consists of' (Saint-Denis 1960: 101). The exercises that follow are, therefore, not simply intended to assist you in developing a role within a play. Instead, they offer you quite profound challenges. Deprived of speech and plunged into responding intuitively, you will be unable to hide behind words or prepared clichés and must confront the nature of the stimulus and of your own creative responses front on.

Preparation

> To begin with, the student in improvisation classes is dressed in his practice costume. He is as naked as possible. He has to conquer his self-consciousness. We can see his body at work with all its qualities and defects. He has no scenery. Nothing on stage but a few stools if he wants them.
>
> (Saint-Denis 1960: 102)

Preparation for this kind of improvisation has to involve you in opening yourself up to a form of creative 'exposure'. Your body must be presented as simply as possible – it is recommended that the outfit warn is close fitting, unrestricting, and monochrome. Traditionally drama students have worn black tights and t-shirts for this work. Hair should be drawn back from the face and other accessories (earrings, watches and so on) removed. The improvisations should take place soon after the warm-up activities in order to ensure good physical preparation.

SILENT IMPROVISATION

Context: Copeau and Bing realised that the student actor would too often escape from the demands of an improvisation or game through resorting to words. The use of silence was key to directing the student's attention towards the central emotional and physical core of a person's interaction with the world. The exercises are simple, leaving no complex interpretative decisions for you to hide behind. You are pushed into finding the central action within the scene – what does the person or being confronted with this situation literally 'do'. Props are also removed, so that you are completely focussed on your own movements, gestures and physicality. This is one series of activities for which we have some relatively clear guidelines from records of the original work:

Exercise 4.1

Follow the sequence below (Copeau 1990: 33). Focus on avoiding illustrative gestures and the use of silent pantomime to replace words; try instead to engage in the simple physical activity of the task, exploring the physical experience of the actions involved and the complex interplay between what we do and what we feel:

- ➤ A man comes home, finds a letter and reads it; it's about some trouble he is in, a serious difficulty, a misfortune.
- ➤ The same with a letter about a friend.
- ➤ The same with a letter about someone to whom the reader is indifferent.
- ➤ A man is waiting for a woman who is late for their date.
- ➤ A woman, same action, same time.
- ➤ A man comes home (show his every-day face, what his present feelings are).

Whatever you do, you cannot help but communicate something about your state of mind to those watching – the exercise introduces you to the need to control that process. If you are watching someone else do this exercise, watch carefully to see how effectively they explore the way in which the rhythm, size, weight, and focus of their gestures and movements communicate to the audience. Notice how quickly they can fall into the need to 'act' rather than to 'do' the scene – the temptation to entertain rather than explore the truth of the situation can be very strong.

To watch for

Copeau identified two particular qualities to observe in this exercise: 'discontinuous actions which seem to be intentional, artificial, theatrical, and the continuous actions which give an impression of portentousness and inner sincerity, real life and power.' (ibid.: 34). It is not exactly clear what is meant by 'discontinuous' and 'continuous', but we might conjecture that Copeau is encouraging you to identify actions which are consistent with an inner sense of purpose and intention, and those which are fragmented and abrupt responses intended to make an effect. Throughout, the emphasis is on the gentle encouragement of emotion through action rather than the forcing of emotion in order to cover empty actions, devoid of intention and impulse.

EXPLORING THE EMOTIONS

Context: The Vieux-Colombier's performance in *Les Fourberies de Scapin* was praised for the physical and emotional vitality of the young company. The emotions seemed sincere and believable, and yet at the same time there was a playfulness and delight in the actors' work. The exercise below indicates how this attitude to the playing of emotions was embedded into the Vieux-Colombier's training regimes.

Exercise 4.2

➤ 'Express a feeling or an emotion with the face only, very rapidly; to be guessed at by the others' (ibid.). The aim of this exercise should not be an empty technical virtuosity; you must avoid *cabotinage*. Instead treat the exercise like a game, and learn to 'play' your emotions without losing sincerity and commitment. You must strive to find the impulse which creates the face. An audience can help by giving clear critical feedback – they must report honestly whether the emotion is genuinely conveyed or just indicated.

➤ 'With the back turned – astonishment, anxiety, depression, anger, sorrow, returning courage and hope' (ibid.). Your back acts as a form of mask. It cannot speak, it cannot mime, it must find the rhythms, tensions and dynamics which both generate and convey the relevant state.

➤ 'The beginning of an emotion, a feeling or a thought, developing through to the end.' (ibid.). Standing in a line of at least five or six people, face out to front. Work on one chosen emotion at a time.

Starting at one end of the line, someone begins by searching for a subtle and restrained physical expression of the emotion (sadness, fear, laughter, anger). They then turn to the person next to them who turns to them and looks at the level they are 'presenting'. At this stage the emotion is passed on, the next person using the impetus from the first to create the same emotion which they take into themselves, accentuate slightly, and pass on to the next person. The process passes back and forth along the line until the emotion has reached its peak and then back and forth again as it diminishes towards neutral. The participants learn to play the rhythms of emotions, thoughts and feelings – sensing the physical 'life' of a thought/emotion/feeling.

Developments

➤ When the emotion reaches a suitable peak (or trough) allow it to transform. Find the point, for instance, at which howls of laughter turn into wails of sadness, or vice-versa.

➤ Break up the line, but know the order in which you pass the emotion. Take part in a simple group activity, during which you allow the emotion to build, diminish and transform (e.g. laying a table, making a bed, putting up a tent).

➤ Repeat as above, but without a set order for passing the emotion, allow it to grow and change organically.

➤ Explore how such an exercise might work within the demands of a scripted scene. Possible scenes might include: the lovers' quarrelling in Act 3 Scene 2 of *A Midsummer Night's Dream*; the slow gloom that settles over Act 4 of Chekhov's *Three Sisters*; or, the growing panic as the townspeople await the arrival of the inspector in Act 1 of Gogol's *The Government Inspector*.

To watch for

As well as an exercise to develop a sense of the improvised play of emotions, this is also a group exercise which develops group awareness and ensemble playing. Do not use this as an excuse for individual emoting. By the same token, this is not just a technical exercise, for the expression of the emotion to work you need to find ways to 'fill' the emotion, to make it real. What is surprising is the extent to which the rest of the group can help in this – sustaining the impulse for the emotion within the group.

IMAGINATIVE PLAY

> [I]t is from games that we would like to construct, not a system, but an experiential education. We would like to develop the child, without distorting his development, by the means that he himself provides, towards which he himself feels the greatest inclination, through play, in play, through games which are noticeably structured and heightened.
>
> (Copeau in Rudlin 1986: 44)

Context: From watching the play of the younger pupils at the school, Copeau and Bing saw the potential value of imaginative play in developing the actor's skills and abilities. Bing seems intuitively to have understood how the pupils' play could be gently developed into dramatic improvisation (Donahue 1998: 66). For Copeau, play subverts intellectualism and artificiality. Using games and play as a starting point also allowed the students to enter with greater ease into the physicality of the work. Bing had observed how students had responded when Copeau had read for them, their delight in and enthusiasm for acting out the tales and stories they heard. The children used what came to hand and Bing, fascinated, realised that their play offered a model for the development of imaginative and creative improvisation. Such improvisation games have become common in theatre teaching and workshops, and their familiarity has meant that participants are often complacent about such simple and well-known games. The challenge for you in trying out such exercises is to remove the clichés which have accumulated around them, and find a way of enabling yourself to return to the basic challenges at the core of this work – energising your own theatrical play within the associations your imagination can bring forward from the world with which you engage.

Preparation

Choose several simple objects (paintbrush, umbrella, broom, hammer – the sort of things which are everyday objects, generally familiar to the exercise participants). Place the objects in a space and establish clear boundaries. Identify the space as an area for play and experiment, a place where objects can take on dream-like qualities, where they can change their properties and be used in unusual ways. You may drop in and out of the exercise by leaving the space, but the objects must always remain in the space.

Exercise 4.3

➤ Move through the space using objects as you feel the urge. Allow yourself to interact with others when it happens, as this will reinforce the imaginative use of the objects, aiding you to integrate the objects into dramatic play.

➤ Allow the improvisation to last for a significant period of time. This will allow obvious uses of the objects to be worked out. Avoid the standard format for this kind of exercise where the group sit in a circle and participants have to take it in turns to 'play' with the object. This tends to transform the exercise into a task to be got out of the way as soon as possible; panic takes over from imagination, with anxiety growing as each person's turn approaches.

Developments

➤ Careful selection of the objects to be used may create a background theme (carpentry, seafaring, bourgeois, domestic). Does this affect the nature of the play? Can it create provocative and interesting contrasts between the objects and the stories created with them?

➤ Existing stories may be chosen which participants explore and enact using the objects. They may explore extracts which interest them at first. Later work could focus on drawing together improvised work into a more structured enactment.

➤ The objects may be mimed. Start by preparing a mimed action with an 'invisible' object. When that is done, work to find a moment when both the action and the object can transform smoothly into another object and another action. Perhaps you might start brushing the floor with an imaginary broom, which then transforms seamlessly into digging the earth with a spade.

➤ Next scenes can be set up, stories begun, and then the 'invisible' objects used, are allowed to change and transform, allowing one scene to dissolve and cross-fade into another.

ANIMAL IMPROVISATION

Context: The improvisation work on animals began with Copeau and Suzanne Bing's first experiments with the idea of a Vieux-Colombier school in 1916. Suzanne Bing developed the animal improvisation process further during her exploration of children's games at Margaret Naumburg's school during the New York tour. On return to Paris, Bing used pictures of animals as stimuli to create 'animal characters', leading to the use of zoo visits to promote detailed observation and imitation of animal characteristics (Kusler 1979: 21). Animal work offered the opportunity to develop several important aspects of the School's pedagogy at the same time: examination of the dynamics of the natural world; challenging of the student's imaginative resources; exploration of the potential for self-transformation; development of the student's physical skills and control; and, subversion of the inhibiting influence of the intellect. Essentially you are learning about character through the imaginative exploration of mind and body, based on a strong external stimulus. For Copeau this represented an ideal preparation for the task of acting – encouraging selflessness, transformation, close observation, respect for the source, and imaginative play.

Preparation

Research: Where at all possible, it is certainly desirable to arrange a visit to a Zoo or similar animal sanctuary as a preliminary stage to work on animal improvisations. You will benefit immeasurably from the opportunity to study animals 'in the flesh' prior to: a) making your choice of animal, and b) commencing the improvisations. The choice of course is vast – fish, birds, mammals, reptiles, insects – and perhaps a little daunting at first. You will however feel instinctively drawn to certain animals, and this should certainly inform your decision. It is also valuable to get the opinions of others, to share observations, and to consider possible affinities in relation to physique, emotional qualities and vocality. Having chosen your animal:

- Observe the animal closely (or attempt to recall the animal through memory in as much detail as you can). This is an important period of personal research which you should undertake with care and diligence.
- What is the animal's habitual environment – wet, dry, damp? Cold, hot or temperate? Is it most comfortable on the wing, amongst the tree-tops, in caves or underground hollows, in the dark, on wide open spaces, or amongst trees and long grass?
- Consider the movement qualities of the animal – how does it walk, sit, stand, and run? Where is its weight, and how does it carry it? Is it light or heavy, quick or slow, sinuous and evasive or direct and forceful? How does the animal walk, with what weight, with what

tread? Does it stroll, run, slither, prowl, strut, or scamper? What are the rhythms of its movement – regular or abrupt, rapid or slow?

- Observe the inter-relationship between the head, the spine, and the limbs. What leads the animal – its head, its nose, its beak, its chest, or its legs? How much flexibility does the spine have? If the animal has a tail, how is the use and movement of the tail related to the animal's poise, grace, and speed?

- Notice the animal's breath – how does this relate to its physical rhythms? To its physical presence? How does its breath punctuate and/or sustain its movements. Does it pant, or taste the air with its tongue? How does its breath relate to the sounds it makes – growls, purrs, cries, gasps or hisses for example?

- Notice how the animal's intention is evident through the whole of their body and their movement, it is as if they think with their body. Where is their focus – all around them, on a fixed point or one specific place/object, on themselves? What are its needs, and how are they evidenced in its movement, posture, and focus – self-defence, protection, food, reproduction, or play? How does it eat and drink?

- Is the sex of the animal important – how does it relate with others of the same sex, or of the opposite sex? Is it a herd/flock/pack animal or a loner? How does it interact with other animals – is the use of the face important, is physique related to social dominance? How much space does it need? How is social status established, displayed, and maintained?

From research to practice: Observation then needs to be followed by physical experimentation. There are numerous approaches to animal improvisation and the process laid out below is just one. Experiment and find what works best for you, but try not to let the exercise become too obsessed with detail at the expense of your imaginative engagement with the task. Always remember that a key challenge for you is truthfulness to the original stimuli – you cannot change the animal to your liking, you must seek to enter its world on its terms.

Before you begin to improvise insure that the space is clean and that you will not be interrupted. It is important that you do not feel inhibited or anxious about being seen by others not involved in the process. Concentration and focus is very important.

Exercise 4.4

➤ Find a bit of space where you can begin to work on your animal. For the first stages of the work you should not interact with other 'animal-improvisers'. Your focus must be on your own work, and the diversity of 'animals' in the space can be a distraction from the quality of your own work.

➤ First imagine your animal sleeping. Observe the sleeping animal in your imagination for a few minutes, then at your own speed allow your body to adapt into a position which feels aligned with the animal's sleeping body-position. Sense how your spine can adapt to the spinal alignment of the animal, how your weight can settle like that of the animal, how your breath can match its own, how its rhythms can inform your own.

➤ The moment of waking is a crucial point of transition for the animal, and one which richly rewards the quality of attention you give it. It is this moment that reveals so much about the animal's relationship to its environment, to its fellow creatures and to its self. There are several stages to explore: the initial coming to consciousness, stretching and re-invigorating the body, grooming and cleaning, and moving off. The most difficult aspect of this exercise is the look of the animal's eyes. The eyes of an animal are alert and focussed, but they lack the self-awareness of the conscious human gaze. This is hard to describe, but you will recognise the difference easily when you see it. You need to work on 'deadening' your eyes a little – as an animal you see to react to things, not to know them and understand them in the way that humans do.

➤ Waking can be followed by movement around the space, exploring how the creature moves when comfortable, frightened, playing or at speed. Try to sustain the improvisation for at least twenty to thirty minutes – it is possible for such work to continue at a high level of concentration and engagement for an hour or so. It is an excellent exercise for developing sustained concentration, physical discipline, and for learning how to hold yourself within an imagined situation for a relatively long period of time.

Developments

➤ Explore the relationships between groups of animals: chickens all clucking around the farmyard together; chimpanzees grooming each other; puppies playing with older dogs; snakes slithering over each other; vultures squabbling over a carcass.

➤ Explore the relationship between carefully chosen kinds of contrasting animal: a dog and a cat; a snake and a vulture; a flock of birds and a crocodile. Try to be careful of falling too quickly into easy and stereotypical inter-relations.

➤ Create your own animal display (a zoo, a safari park, a forest, an ocean, or a jungle) and invite an audience in to view it. Resist the temptation to 'entertain' the audience – your task is first and foremost to convince them.

➤ Develop the animal you have worked on into a human character. Begin by improvising as the animal, and then gradually start to develop towards a human representation. As far as is possible, within a human frame, maintain the animal's sense of weight, rhythm, posture, breath, focus, and need. Think of your creation as half-human and half-animal. Now explore this character's movement, posture, interaction, voice, social status and use of space. As a further development you might see how far you can reduce the sense of the animal without losing it entirely within the human. This kind of work can lead usefully into preparation for characters in both devised and scripted performances – plays such as Ben Jonson's *Volpone* or Edward Albee's *Zoo Story* might be excellent texts to use for further exploration of this work.

Copeau extended the animal improvisation into work which made direct use of the skills acquired. One proposed study for his students was to adapt scenes from **La Fountaine**'s *Fables* (Copeau 1990: 34–5).

Jean de La Fountaine (1621–1695) was an eminent French writer who published several collections of stories and fables in 'free verse' between 1664 and 1694. The fables used stories about animals to satirise human behaviour.

Other texts which might be interesting to study in this way include:

* George Orwell's *Animal Farm*;
* Peter Brook's adaptation of *The Conference of the Birds*;

- Edward Albee's *Zoo Story*;
- Ben Johnson's *Volpone*.

MASK-WORK

> With the mask, it is impossible to cheat. When we try to express a feeling or an emotion, if we do not feel impelled by an interior force, we know that we're not 'with it'. Every contrived gesture was a false note; wearing masks taught us also to be sincere.
>
> (Jean Dasté in Leabhart 2004: 321)

Copeau wanted to train actors to achieve a vibrant and theatrical sincerity. Acting involves a dual tension for the actor, who must respect the inherent pretence of theatre whilst creating a performance that is sincere and believable. The mask is an ideal tool for the exploration of this dichotomy. it is a symbol of theatricality, and at the same time it reflects back to the actor any artificiality or mannerisms. The mask is an overtly theatrical tool, able to force the actor to engage physically with his or her actions, emotions and intentions, and to exteriorise them, making the inner conflicts of the drama part of the physical action. At the same time, as Leabhart (1995) suggests, the mask is also a tool through which the actor can tap into ritual and shamanic energies. Copeau never sought to overplay this aspect of the mask's power, perhaps because its origins lie in a paganism which, latterly, his own Christianity found hard to accept. Nonetheless he was willing to acknowledge the profound effect the mask could have on both the wearer and the spectator.

BEGINNING MASK-WORK: THE NEUTRAL MASK

> I think that there is, as a point of departure, a kind of purity, a wholeness of the individual, a state of calm, of naturalness, of relaxation
>
> (Copeau in Leabhart 2004: 324).

For Copeau, the 'noble' or 'neutral' mask marked the 'point of departure' for the actor. The neutral mask operated on a number of levels:

- purifying and simplifying gesture and movement;
- giving gesture and movement 'density' and significance;
- creating the need for physical, rather than facial, expression;

- embodying the relationship between immobility and action;
- focussing the performance of simple physical actions – walking, sitting, standing, and simple tasks;
- allowing silent improvisations to develop beyond the everyday and explore atmospheres, places, times of year.

Initially Copeau's students wore stockings over their heads and faces – this partially obscured their facial features, restricting the effectiveness of any facial expressions. It also forced the student to focus more intently on the dramatic effects of their posture and their movement. You might consider exploring this as a simple alternative to purchasing or constructing neutral masks. Later masks were constructed using 'papier-mâché, shellac and flour, linen and glue' (Donahue 1998: 69). These masks were sturdier and more robust, but perhaps more importantly the elimination of distinctive features could be explored with greater subtlety and varied to greater effect. Marie-Hélène's notes relate how students experienced, 'a force and a new security – a sort of sense of balance and an awareness of each gesture and of themselves' (Marie-Hélène Copeau in Donahue 1998: 69, author's translation).

'SHOEING THE MASK'

A mask is a concrete object. When you put it on your face you receive from it a strong impulse which you have got to obey.

(Saint-Denis 1960: 103)

Context: The first stage of Copeau's mask-work focuses on putting the mask on. This is not just about physical preparation, but about getting into a mental state which allows the mask to 'work upon' the actor. One of Copeau's pupil's, Jean Dorcy, describes how students were taught to 'shoe' the mask (Dorcy 1961: 108–9). The instructions below are adapted from Dorcy's description:

Exercise 4.5

➤ Sit comfortably and upright in the middle of a chair, not leaning against the back of the seat. Have the sense of balancing your spine and head on the 'sitting bones' of your pelvis. Your legs should be spaced just wide enough to ensure good balance when you stand (i.e. about hip width apart), and your feet should be flat on the ground. In this position, the body is relaxed, poised, and ready for action.

➤ Holding the mask by its elastic or strap, stretch the right arm out at shoulder height. The left hand, also stretched out, helps to 'shoe' the mask, thumb holding the chin, index and second finger seizing the opening of the mouth. Slip the mask onto the face, with the strap going behind the head.

➤ As you 'shoe' the mask, inhale, and close the eyes.

➤ In doing this, keep everything else still. Just use your hands and arms to ensure that the mask fits comfortably and securely, and that hair is properly arranged (it is useful to move the hair over the strap, once in place).

➤ At the same time, breathe and place your forearms and hands on the thighs. The arms, as well as the elbows, touch the torso, fingers not quite reaching the knees.

➤ Now open the eyes and inhale. Then, in one movement, close the eyes, exhale and bend the head forward, allowing the back to round slightly. Keep your arms, hands, torso, and head completely relaxed.

➤ Try to clear your mind. Allow your thoughts to float, and do not focus on any one thing. If it helps, repeat silently or out loud a simple phrase (Dorcy suggests: 'I am not thinking of anything, I am not thinking of anything ...').

➤ If this clearing process is not successful Dorcy also suggests concentrating on the soft dark colour shades found inside the eye.

➤ Simultaneously, inhale and sit upright, then exhale and open your eyes.

Things to watch for

➤ It may be tempting to look in a mirror to see how you look in the mask. This is not helpful at this stage and should be avoided. Seeing your reflection brings back your self-consciousness, it opens up for you the gap between what you do and how you look. Try instead to think of emptying and simplifying, of identifying with the mask. Let the mask work to focus your attention on the impulse to action and the efficiency of movement which its neutrality invokes.

➤ The breath is very important – avoid breathing mechanically, or holding your breath unnecessarily, throughout this exercise. It is the breath that helps the mask live. Notice how the focus moves between inner contemplation and awareness of the environment.

These shifts are linked to the breath – its rhythms and its dynamics.
➤ This exercise was used for the 'shoeing' of the neutral mask, but the same technique can help with the 'shoeing' of expressive, abstract, or character masks.
➤ As you become more experienced you may be tempted to short-cut this process. Examine carefully what happens if you do so – are you as aware of the inner and outer spaces, do you feel as centred and composed, do you feel as connected with the mask? How does the 'shoeing' process help to prepare and focus you for the work to come? Does it have any effect on the nature of your 'performance state', the level of consciousness within which you function as you perform? There appears to be an intentionally ritualistic element to this process, a sense in which the actor is tapping into a heightened state of awareness and concentration. Masks have of course often been associated with the achievement of these kinds of states (see Leabhart 1995).

Before you begin to work with the neutral mask it can be valuable to consider a few important guidelines:

➤ Try not to touch the mask – it draws unnecessary attention to the mask's artificiality.
➤ By the same token, avoid trying to speak when wearing the mask. Likewise avoid gestural pantomime as a poor substitute for speech.
➤ Be aware of what your body is doing. Aimless fidgeting and unfocused movement stops the mask from coming alive, tending to reveal the wearer's discomfort and not the mask's own qualities – 'masks dislike agitation, … they can only be animated by controlled, strong, and utterly simple actions which depend upon the richness of the inner life within the calm and balanced body of the performer' (Saint-Denis 1960: 104).
➤ Remember that a mask works for the spectator when it is visible.
➤ Do not get over-awed by the mask – it is a tool for the imagination, a conduit through which to channel your sense of play.

NEUTRAL MASK IMPROVISATIONS

Context: According to Mira Felner, the first silent, full-face mask exercises focused on 'simple explorations of emotional states: "Tiredness, hunger, sunworship, fear," among others' (Felner 1985: 45). Copeau's aim was to encourage emotional expression and to break down inhibitions. The work centred initially on natural elements improvised in neutral masks, but this eventually evolved into work towards characterisation. The use of the neutral mask forces the actor to move beyond an easy reliance on words or facial expressions, the relevant state has to be physically embodied. This embodiment must also be more than a pantomimic representation; it needs to be a deeply physical identification with the required state of being. For hunger, avoid rubbing the stomach; for tiredness, wiping the weary brow. These are exactly the sorts of clichés that Copeau wanted to remove from the theatre.

Solo improvisations

Simon Murray describes some neutral mask exercises in his book on Jacques Lecoq's work (Murray 2003), and Sears Eldredge outlines a programme of neutral mask training in his book *Mask Improvisation for Actor Training and Performance* (1996). Certainly some of these exercises clearly owe an important debt to Copeau's ideas for the neutral mask. Just as Lecoq gradually introduces the neutral mask into situations where they must respond physically to a natural environment (ibid.: 75), so too, Copeau developed neutral mask scenarios which challenged the student to discover the physical rhythms and dynamics of the environment they engaged with. Thomas Leabhart describes how students would start off by improvising simple actions – 'a man trying to shoo away a fly; a woman strangling a fortune-teller; actions used in trade; a sequence of movements made by a machine' (Leabhart 1989: 26). As the students progressed Copeau would give them time for a brief meeting to discuss their response to the theme, at other times he would give the stimulus and 'the students would attempt, without reflection, to express what was suggested to them by that word' (ibid.: 27). Try the following themes as solo improvisations.

Exercise 4.6

'Shoe' the mask. Stand in a neutral posture and become aware of your breathing. Enter the space and, using movement, try to encapsulate the essence of one of the themes below in movement.

➤ Summer
➤ The city
➤ The farewell.

Things to consider

➤ Constantly monitor your work for clichés.
➤ Avoid pantomimic responses – picking flowers, looking at imaginary watches, etc.
➤ Try to avoid over-complicating – be open to the simple responses.
➤ Feel for the rhythm of the environment, and how that might change and develop.
➤ Allow yourself to play with the theme – move between naturalistic and abstract responses.
➤ Remember – this exercise is about discovery and experiment, not end result.
➤ What difference does it make whether you give yourself any time to plan beforehand?
➤ What things do you discover about the theme itself?

Group improvisations

Below is an original example of a group exercise, recorded by Waldo Frank when he observed some of Copeau's classes. You could explore this improvisation using the neutral mask. You will need a group of fellow actors to work with – four or five should be enough.

Exercise 4.7

Read the theme below. Decide whether to discuss it before beginning or not. Prepare yourselves by 'shoeing' the mask, and be sensitive to when all performers are ready to begin.

> A strand, fisherfolk look out at a stormy sea, a rowboat arrives, the seamen leave the boat and go to the fisherfolk with news of the drowning of a comrade, the scene shifts to inside a fisher cottage, the wife and children await the father, the friends come in with the sad news (Kusler 1979: 45).

- ➤ Enter the space and gather in the opening positions you have decided on.
- ➤ After you have attempted the whole scenario, break it down and work on each section in turn.

Things to watch for
- ➤ Notice the points at which the mood and atmosphere of each section 'turns'.
- ➤ Consider how the relationship with the environment changes and explore how this can be expressed through movement.
- ➤ Waldo Frank noticed that the original students made subtle use of rhythm, and were alert to the 'socially dimensioned fullness' of the scenario (Frank in Felner 1985: 46). How are the different social relationships made clear through your movement – the working people on the beach, the seamen arriving, the family in the cottage?

In both the solo and the group improvisation exercises you will need to find a subtle balance between conscious control and imaginative release. Leabhart (2004) discusses at some length the 'trance' effect of mask-work, a quality which he feels is central to Copeau's work. But he also picks up on what Dasté calls a 'doubled' consciousness – where the actor is both in control and not in control. My own experience of neutral mask improvisation confirms for me complexity of this relationship. Do not be concerned if you do not find this balance easy to establish at the first attempt. This kind of mask-work is however about training for performance and not about psychotherapy. You should heed the words of Jean Dorcy who advises the actor that, 'above all, even in the depths of trance he experiences, he must not lose sight of the general structure of the improvisation' (Jean Dorcy in Leabhart 2004: 325).

Slow motion and the neutral mask

The manner of playing resembled the slow motion of film. But while that is the slowing down of fragments of reality, ours was the slow production of one gesture in which many others were synthesised.

(Decroux in Leabhart 1989: 27)

Context: Decroux, a student at the Vieux-Colombier School for a period, was struck by the expressive control the students sought to achieve. The changes from slow-motion to explosive movement to immobility were all used to powerful dramatic effect, making a musicality of the actors' movement (Leabhart 1989: 28). Copeau believed that immobility and slow-motion gave 'density' to the students' work. This kind of movement study was applied to best effect in the students' 1924 presentation of the Nōh play *Kantan* directed by Suzanne Bing.

Exercise 4.8

➤ Begin by taking simple movements around the space – walking, running, sitting, and so on – and vary the speed at which you do them. Go from normal speed, to slow motion, to immobility, and to fast. Consider what qualities this gives the movement, what dramatic effects are achieved.

➤ Take specific exercises outlined above and explore at which moments slow motion and immobility might be used. Again, reflect on the dramatic effect – how are gestures and movements effected, how are relationships between performers affected?

➤ How long can slow-motion or immobility be sustained for? With and without the use of the mask?

➤ You might also want to try out the effect of fast-motion, and its effects on the exercises.

Developments

➤ These experiments could also be used on texts – exploring the rhythmic dynamics of comedies, tragedies and melodramas, for instance.

A NEW COMMEDIA

Context: The neutral mask has limited dramatic appeal outside the classroom. It is principally a teaching tool and, although it is an invaluable part of the student actor's learning journey, it has seldom been used effectively in performance. Working with the neutral mask does however give a useful preparation for the discipline and control needed for mask-work (and for acting) in general. If you have already completed all the exercises outlined above, you will have built up some valuable knowledge and skills. Copeau's work on a *new commedia* offers a fascinating opportunity to bring these new skills to bear on the creation of dramatic material.

Exercise 4.9

Using the work you have already done, you can now choose to work on some of the projects outlined below. Each of these exercises can be used to develop the character of a half-mask. You may be working with a ready-made mask, or with one you have made yourself; in either case you must treat the mask as something that needs to be explored and try to allow the character to emerge, emptying your mind of any ideas you had when making the mask. Alternatively you might find some of these exercises useful as preliminary stages to the designing and manufacture of a mask.

➤ Take a selection of animal-characters, characters you have developed from animal studies. Develop each individually – take it in turns to watch each working in their habitual spaces, interview them, and place them in relevant contexts.

> In the New Comedy, comparison of the characters of certain types with the appearance of certain animals.
>
> (Copeau 1990: 34–5)

➤ Look for possible interesting locations/situations which would enable two or more of these characters to meet and interact. Observe carefully and note any possible narratives which develop. Take care not to lose the heightened physicality. You may wish to develop half or full masks which help to draw out some of the animal people's characteristics. Allow talk, but avoid chatter for the sake of it, think of words as actions. If this proves problematic, then use *grummelotage* or 'gobbledy-gook' – make up words, perhaps based on the sounds of your source animal.

> *Grummelotage*, or improvised meaningless dialogue – 'the music of meaning'.
>
> (Saint-Denis 1982: 168)

➤ List contemporary character types – be careful not to make simplistic assumptions, it can be useful to consider the significance of different types across conventional boundaries of gender, class, ethnicity, dis/ability. Identify key costume items, observe typical postures, reactions and habits of behaviour.

➤ Search for the physical 'signatures' of each character type.

Developments

➤ When you are beginning to get a sense of the mask's character, start to explore how costumes and props might help with moving them on.

➤ Inevitably the work starts with few words – as you gain in confidence explore what kind of talk will suit the mask. Think about the tone, timbre and pitch of the voice, where it is centred in the body, how the voice is used.

➤ If you are working with others, look for masks which work well together – allow small groupings to emerge, and explore their dramatic potential. This can lead to the beginnings of short scenarios.

MAKING YOUR OWN MASKS

Copeau encouraged his student actors to explore the skills involved in mask making. Mask-making is a hands-on activity which develops a tactile and sensory understanding of the interaction between materials, face and expression. If you wish to make your own masks it is advisable at first to get advice from someone who has some experience in mask-making techniques – instructions in books are useful, but working with sticky materials and turning pages at the same time can be a messy business! It is possible to purchase very good quality ready-made masks, and national or regional mime and physical theatre associations, such as Total Theatre Network in the United Kingdom, are good sources of information regarding suppliers and manufacturers.

A simple neutral mask can be made by taking a cast of your own face, the features of which can be smoothed as further layers of material are added. Suitable materials can include strips of plaster-soaked fabric (gypsona), gummed paper, even papier-mâché. Masks can be made by applying suitable materials to the wearer's face, but care must be taken to ensure that adequate vents for breathing are provided and that the face is well lubricated in order to avoid damage to the skin and facial hair (strips of tissue paper are useful for covering eyebrows and eyelids) and to facilitate the removal of the mask once the materials are set enough. Professional quality masks are made from durable synthetic materials (which can be sweaty and hot to use) or from leather (a traditional material, more pleasant to wear, but expensive). These can be constructed off a plaster cast of your face for a comfortable fit.

THE CHORUS

An 'ensemblier', according to the dictionary, is 'an artist who aims at unity of general effect'. We were 'ensembliers'. We set out to develop initiative, freedom, and a sense of responsibility in the individual, as long as he or she was ready or able to merge his personal qualities into the ensemble.

(Saint-Denis 1960: 92)

ACTING TOGETHER

Context: The Chorus was, as we have already seen, a core element of Copeau's *mise-en-scène*. As well as representing a powerful dramatic effect, choral expression also embodied the kind of intuitive communion which Copeau valued so highly in performers. The exercises in the School allowed Copeau to explore this work in detail (Rudlin 2000: 60–1).

Preparation

Chorus work requires group sensitivity and awareness. It is useful to work with people who you already know, if this is not possible emphasis must be put on concentration and peripheral vision, and participants must let go of the desire to 'lead' the group. Group exercises take time, it is not possible to build a sense of communion and unity quickly. The exercises outlined below could easily form an extended session of several hours, or be developed over several days. It is also important to develop the exercise beyond simple copying and following, what Michel Saint-Denis calls 'the herd instinct' (Saint-Denis 1982: 164), which can deaden the work and lead to a fascistic feel quite out of line with Copeau's intentions. To work as a group, as an ensemble, it is necessary to develop a strong sense of space, what Michel Saint-Denis calls a 'memory of space' (ibid.: 165), and to allow emotion to be transmitted spontaneously and visibly within the group.

Exercise 4.10

➤ Start in pairs. Agree who will be the leader and who will follow. The leader begins moving; they can move all around the space, high and low, fast and slow, doing abstract or everyday actions, gestures and movements. The follower copies the leader as closely as possible. Try not to catch your partner out, but to develop a rapport between you both – challenge them when necessary, don't let the process become predictable. Swap over, and repeat. Then try with the leadership changing smoothly and frequently – sensing intuitively when it is right to lead and when to follow.

➤ Combine into small groups of about four or five. Form a diamond shape, within which a leader is always easily visible no matter in which direction the whole group faces. One member leads and the others follow. The group can move off around the space. Interaction with other groups may happen, but all in silence and using choral movement. Again try to establish a strong sense of group movement. Change over leadership, explore different kinds of movement. Finally try to allow the leadership to change when it needs to. Groups can build up, and/or reduce. Allow the distance between group members to increase and to decrease, but try and keep the same 'connectedness'.

➤ Try to follow the leader's movements as closely as possible. Follow their actions, gestures, the little movements of their hands, their breathing. Try to get a sense of when the leader is about to stop or move off.

➤ As the group turns and changes direction, allow the leadership to change. Try to make the transition as smooth as possible.

➤ It is common for groups to look very self-conscious at first as they rather obviously observe each other closely and find the concentration level difficult. Try to disguise the leader, try to make it look as if you have been practising for a long time. Accept imperfect imitation if the impulse and the intention to move can be closely followed.

Developments

➤ Allow groups to join up. Bigger groups demand more concentration, but the dramatic effect is stronger. Try with one leader, and then with changing leaders.

➤ Now, in the same groups, keeping the same sense of

'connectedness', let the group move and gesture only in sympathy with the leader – that is to say that they do not need to copy the leader exactly, but to identify the nature of his or her actions and complement them. This is not the same as improvising whatever you like – the driving force behind the scene is still the leader, the chorus support and build the mood, events, environment suggested by the leader. At the start it may be that someone calls out environments or short narratives as the focus for the work. Later, if the group are working well together, they may intuitively follow each other.

➤ As a group, slowly and silently, and whilst continuing with the exercise, establish a common task which you are undertaking. Copeau's students used activities such as the washing of clothes in a stream, being ferried across a river, laying the table and preparing a meal, harvesting the crop, fishermen and women on the beach, the gathering of a crowd. You may want initially to try out some contemporary themes of your own (e.g. riding on a bus or underground train, supporting a sports team, or working on an assembly line), but work towards allowing the group silently to find its own themes. Variations may now increasingly creep in, but the sense of a shared group activity should remain strong. The group no longer copy exactly the leader's actions and gestures, but work with a sensitivity to the leader's rhythms and impulses.

➤ All the exercises above can be done with or without the use of neutral masks. The use of the masks slightly inhibits your vision, but increases your theatrical presence and heightens your group awareness. Non-masked choral improvisation allows some other developments to be explored:

➤ Consider the possibility of song in the group activities (it might be useful to use choral singing in the early warm-ups and preparation – perhaps a range of suitable songs could be learnt over time). Who leads the singing? Does everyone sing all the time? At what volume? What songs, melodies or sounds might be used?

➤ Encourage the group to explore changes of rhythm within the activity – how does this effect the mood conveyed. Possible rhythmic changes might include: slowing down, speeding up, slowing down then speeding up, speeding up then slowing down, and stopping for a few seconds. Do changes in posture have similar effects? Changes in group focus – close, distant, shifting from one person to another person, looking at nobody? Explore how the group activity might change in response to a particular event – an arrival, a departure, a significant sound (a gunshot, a bell, sobbing) or sight (a distant light, a flag raised, a ship on the horizon).

➤ Try to improvise sounds and words or speech. This is much harder than it might seem. The temptation is to embellish the drama with narrative rather than consolidate the group cohesion and the sense of mood, place and time. You will soon sense that idol chatter feels very out of place and that genuine speech comes from a physical impulse to speak related to the activity you are doing. It can be useful to start with improvised sound that is 'meaningful' to the performer, but inarticulate to the audience. In this way vocal sound can be used to reveal the mood of the group, and later perhaps lead into speech (see Saint-Denis 1960: 105). Vocal sound effects may be another appropriate way to develop the work further.

➤ Explore group transformations – how can a group activity change all at once and smoothly. Who signals the change? This will take practice to do and works most effectively as something you set yourselves to explore over a period of as much as fifteen or twenty minutes. The aim should be to find a transformation which is communicated purely through the group's movement, posture and positions in the space, and that happens so smoothly that the audience are not aware of the change coming (see Copeau 1990: 46–7 for an example of a choral scene moving from a beach to a fisherman's hut).

➤ Finally, devise a group scenario. Michel Saint-Denis (1982) suggests titles such as 'The Crossing of the Red Sea', a mining disaster, a shipwreck, a labour strike or a lockout, war, exodus, floods – titles which resonated with meaning for the times in which he was writing. You may want try these or you may prefer to create your own titles. Music can be a good additional stimulus – have a range of recorded music available for you to experiment with and choose from. Try to ensure that the group remains the protagonist of the action and not any one individual. It is only a short step from this to work on text, one possible scene for such an exercise might be the washing scene (Act 2, Scene 1) from *Yerma* by Frederico Garcia Lorca.

Alternative starting points

➤ Start with a group of five or six standing together, so that you are lightly touching each other and your eyes are closed. In your own time, slowly sway, exploring different directions but always together and in the same direction as each other. The aim is to develop a sense of ensemble movement, such that the swaying motion becomes seamless, continuous, and so that no obvious leader is visible. Sustain the exercise in order to build concentration: it will take time before the intuitive sense of group develops.

➤ Variations – add humming or other soft sounds to the swaying. The sound and the swaying can be slowly and gradually built up until the group rushes out and forward and comes to a stop with a shout. There should not be any external command, the moment to break out and rush forward should be felt through your group rapport. Alternatively the group may slowly begin to move sensing intuitively who is leading and which direction to move in.

➤ As a group imagine you are standing in a small boat (Saint-Denis (1982: 166) originally suggested a simple ferry boat). Sense for the movement of the boat on the water, and its particular movement as the ferryman begins to propel the boat across the water. What happens if other boats pass and their wakes rock the ferry.

➤ What happens when a group 'watch a train moving against a far horizon, watch a plane doing stunts, watch race horses passing, watch a tennis match' (ibid.: 167)? How do you respond to what you see? In following what you see, how far do you also become what you see?

THE JOURNEY'S END

The connection between feeling and expression, and the sincerity of that connection, was everything to Copeau and represented the spiritual and moral integrity for which he strove in his work. Nonetheless, he did not concern himself too much with psychology and the actor's inner soul – for Copeau the driving logic of the theatre could not be reduced to psychological realism, theatre had its own poetics which gave a particular shape and dynamics to the expression of emotion and the representation of character. The overall structure of a Copeau-based training is thus a journey of physical experience and discovery, of imagination and play linked to observation and sincerity. For Copeau this was a personal journey, a journey which cannot be made through any other effort 'than that which you are able to make yourself' (Copeau 1974: 108, author's translation). Michel Saint-Denis provides us with a succinct summary:

As the work progresses, [the student] will move from an ABC made up of the representation of actions taken from his (*sic*) daily life like waking up, eating a meal, returning home, dressing and undressing, to moods that are complicated by external circumstances. He will soon begin to experience the need for concentration and observation; he will recognise the importance of emotional memory. He will become aware of the use of space, of rhythm, of the continuity of action. At the same time the exercises he is given to do, however simple they may be, can never be 'naturalistic': the student must find out for himself and by himself how to represent on stage those naturalistic actions which in real life would involve the handling of objects. So, progressing, he will go on to represent people of different crafts seen at their work in characteristic professional activities and then, move on to transformation – into circus types, into animals, even into the world of dreams. The next step will be the invention of a complete scenario with all the details of circumstance necessary to its complete realisation.

(Saint-Denis 1960: 102–3)

5

COPEAU'S LEGACY

The transmission of Copeau's work across time has taken place at least as much through his practice as through his writings. His legacy is thus twofold: on the one hand, a collection of writings on the nature of acting, its pedagogy, and the function and purpose of theatre in a modern society; and, on the other, a significant body of practical expertise and understanding passed on through his pupils and fellow actors. In all respects his legacy has become so pervasive that it is in danger of becoming invisible. This final section aims therefore to identify some of the ways in which Copeau's work has informed European and American theatre practice over the rest of the twentieth century.

Copeau was the father-figure for all who worked with him. If this was a lonely role for him to play, it was one which he chose for himself, which he saw as his own responsibility; 'Don't speak to the man at the wheel,' he would say (Bentley 1950: 49). Throughout his life he sought constantly to raise theatrical activity to the moral, spiritual and aesthetic level of which he thought it was capable. His example was one of integrity, belief and perseverance. In this sense his most immediate legacy was the re-invigoration of the idea of theatre as a unified artform, and of the director and actor as figures of both moral and artistic authority within the theatre. This he bequeathed to his former colleagues and pupils, many of whom went on to become leading figures in the French theatre, so that, 'in the French-speaking world, his influence as a teacher equalled that of Stanislavsky in Russia and America' (Bradby and Williams 1988: 16). Copeau was, as we have seen, passionately aware of the traditions of European theatre, and very much in touch with the developments taking place across the continent during his lifetime. In this respect he did much to re-establish French theatre on the international scene, and to influence theatre practice elsewhere. On a simpler level, many of the practices and principles outlined throughout this book have had a lasting effect on theatre in Europe and America. Copeau's influence can be identified in the development and use of a wide range of theatre techniques and activities; in the introduction to his book on Copeau, John Rudlin identifies a list which includes: 'drama games; improvisation; animal mimicry; ensemble playing; writer-in-residence; commedia dell'arte revival; mime; mask-work; repertoire rather than repertory; community theatre; theatre as communion' (Rudlin 1986: xiv), and this list is by no means exhaustive.

Previous chapters have already dealt with his relationship with some of his early colleagues and associates (for example Louis Jouvet and Charles Dullin), and with their achievements. Other, younger disciples and their own pupils have also left their mark on the French theatre. The list of theatre artists who can trace the history of their practice and principles back to Copeau provides an impressive 'who's who' of twentieth-century theatre.

Jean Dasté (1904–1994) and **Leon Chancerel** (1886–1965) were students of Copeau's and worked with him, most significantly, as members of Les Copiaus. Dasté became an important figure in the training regime, eventually taking over as leader of the School's gymnastic sessions. He married Copeau's daughter, Marie-Hélène, and both were members of the Compagnie des Quinze. Dasté was a strong campaigner for the decentralisation of French theatre, something he followed through in his own directorship of the Comédie de St Etienne. Leon Chancerel eventually left the Copiaus troupe and set up a touring company, Les Comédiens Routiers. Like Dasté, he shared Copeau's commitment to decentralisation, to the discovery of a modern commedia dell'arte, and to a theatre which was popular and accessible.

Etienne Decroux (1898–1991) is credited as being one of the founding figures of modern mime. Decroux was a student with Copeau and worked briefly with Les Copiaus. His intensive study of corporeal mime in collaboration with Jean-Louis Barrault laid the foundations for his lifetime research into mime and his passionate defence of mime as an artform in its own right. His school in the basement of his home in the Paris suburbs sustained his austere and intense vision of the mime. Though his teaching and techniques are often reduced in the popular imagination to the illusion mime made famous by his former pupil, Marcel Marceau (1923–), Decroux offered a vision of mime as, in a sense which Copeau would have appreciated, a form capable of also approaching the spiritual and the abstract through the body.

Jean-Louis Barrault (1910–1994) was probably one of the greatest postwar French actors, whose own influence has been profound, both in France and in Europe. Barrault trained initially with Copeau's former colleague Charles Dullin, and then later worked with Etienne Decroux on the initial development of modern corporeal mime. Barrault applied the spontaneous physicality which he learnt during this period to much of his later work, including his performance as Baptiste in the film *Les Enfants du Paradis* (1944), and his own adaptations of William Faulkner's *As I Lay Dying* (1935) and of *Rabelais* (1969) (from Rabelais' *Gargantua and Pantagruel*). Barrault's work was deeply influenced by Copeau's heritage; at the core of such work, Barrault saw a vital and invigorating professional honesty, a profound craftsmanship, and a genuine musicality.

Antonin Artaud (1896–1948) was another of Dullin's students who was to have a profound effect on the development of late twentieth century theatre. Artaud was a student at Dullin's Atelier from 1921 to 1923, during which period he also became firm friends with Barrault. Where Barrault was the body through which modern physical theatre developed, Artaud was its spirit and soul. Artaud shared much of Copeau's disgust at the commercialisation of theatre and its consequent lack of moral and spiritual purpose during the early decades of the century: 'There are those who go to the theatre as if they were going to a brothel', he declared (Artaud in Hayman 1977: 66). Behind much of Artaud's writing lay a search for purity and spiritual renewal which echoes Copeau's own. Like Copeau, Artaud rejected 'the false and facile theatre of the bourgeois', and sought instead a 'theatre which finds accommodation where it can, theatre conceived as the accomplishment of the purest human desires', agreeing with Copeau that 'the externals of production must be ignored' (ibid.) so that the focus can be redirected towards the inner drama. Where the two disagreed was over the respect due to the script, in fact Artaud attacked Copeau for being subservient to the text. Nonetheless, Artaud's analysis of Copeau's rehearsal technique is insightful and even grudgingly appreciative:

> Jacques Copeau's idea of a theatre consists in subjugating the *mise en scène* to the text, of making it come forth from the text by means of an intelligent twisting of the very text itself. For Jacques Copeau, it is the text and the words which count above all. Thus, he has a Shakespearean concept of gesture, movement, attitudes and décor. In short, this is the submission of theatre to the language of written literature. Nothing more, that was it: afterwards the French theatre followed his lead.
>
> (Artaud in Copeau 1990: 224)

Michel Saint-Denis (1897–1971), Copeau's nephew, has already been identified as an important standard-bearer for his uncle's work. When Les Copiaus dispersed, Saint-Denis founded the Compagnie des Quinze with many of the old troupe who still felt committed to the same ideals. The Compagnie des Quinze achieved international success. By the 1930s critics were quicker to recognise the value of Copeau's vision for a rejuvenated theatre; as one English theatre critic wrote,

> What they do possess, to our admiration, is the ability to give every visual and verbal essential of the theatre – everything that distinguishes theatre from film and spectacle and lifelikeness – at an economic cost that must be trifling and with resources that amount finally to the physical and mental vitality of the individual player.
>
> (Dukes 1931: 716)

The company survived until the early 1930s, at which point Saint-Denis moved to England where he had significant success as a director, including influential productions of *Oedipus Rex* and *Noah*. Both before and after the Second World War Saint-Denis did much to embed Copeau's approaches to theatre into regimes of actor training across Europe and the United States. He was the founder of several leading drama schools including: the Old Vic Theatre School in London, the Juilliard School Drama Division in New York, the National Theatre School of Canada and the École Supérieure d'Art Dramatique in Strasbourg. Saint-Denis was a long-term collaborator with George Devine, the founder of the **English Stage Company** at the Royal Court, and, in 1962, he was invited to become one of the first triumvirate of directors at the **Royal Shakespeare Company** (RSC), working alongside Peter Hall (1930–) and Peter Brook (see below). Peter Hall was enthused by Saint-Denis' belief that, 'Acting was not a trick to be learned and then performed; it was not imitation, but rather revelation of the whole human personality' (Hall in Saint-Denis 1982: 14). And Copeau's commitment to a balance between the classics and modern writing, and to a style of acting that was vital, energetic and physically expressive but that also respected the centrality of the text, has clearly had a fundamental effect on the driving principles of the RSC.

The **English Stage Company** was founded by George Devine in 1956 to provide a home for new writing. Famous productions include the première of John Osbourne's *Look Back in Anger* in 1956. The **Royal Shakespeare Company** (RSC) was founded in 1962 by Peter Hall, in order to establish a dedicated centre for the exploration in performance of the plays of Shakespeare and his contemporaries, and to bring classical acting skills to bear on modern and contemporary texts.

The Group Theatre – Lee Strasberg (1901–1982) and **Harold Clurman** (1901–1980). Copeau's influence extends beyond France and the teaching establishments founded by Michel Saint-Denis. His lecture tour to America in 1917 had a significant effect on the development of the Little Theater Movement, and through this, on the Group Theatre in New York, one of the most important theatre groups in twentieth century America. Harold Clurman attests to the importance of Copeau's lectures and demonstrations in providing an impetus for the founding of the Group Theatre and for their experiments in ensemble acting: 'Copeau's presence in New York [in 1927 to direct *The Brothers Karamazov*] acted as a catalytic agent in bringing Strasberg and myself together with the thought of forming a theatre of our own' (Clurman 1945: 15).

Jacques Lecoq (1921–1999) initially trained as a movement therapist, but after the Second World War he worked as an actor and choreographer with Jean Dasté. Whilst with Dasté he experienced some of the training and techniques developed by Copeau, whose influence he has acknowledged (Murray 2003: 32). Lecoq went on to work in Italy, with the director Georgio Strehler and with the playwright and actor Dario Fo, where he developed an interest in commedia dell'arte. With the mask-maker Amletto Sartori he set about exploring, as Copeau had done before him, the skills and techniques of the commedia actors. In 1956 he returned to Paris where he established a school for mime, movement and theatre which has become internationally famous. His teaching brings together much that is reminiscent of Copeau's School at the Vieux-Colombier – physical education, acrobatics, improvisation, mask-work, experiments in theatre styles such as commedia dell'arte and Greek tragedy, group creation and choral acting. Past students of Lecoq have included Ariane Mnouchkine (Théâtre du Soleil), Simon McBurney (Complicité) and the director and film-maker Julie Taymor (stage version of *The Lion King*).

Peter Brook (1925–) has been a major figure in European theatre for most of the second half of the twentieth century. A colleague of Michel Saint-Denis during the early years of the RSC, Brook's work has shown something of a similar trajectory to that of Copeau. After considerable success and critical acclaim at the RSC, culminating in a world tour of his seminal production of *A Midsummer Night's Dream* in 1970, Brook left the company to set up a centre for theatre research in Paris with a troupe of international actors. Although based in the Théâtre Bouffes du Nord the company have made several journeys into non-western communities (Northern Africa, Iran, India) to explore the nature of theatrical communication across cultures. Brook can be seen as sharing with Copeau a belief in the humanist potential of theatre to communicate across socio-cultural boundaries (Auslander 1997: 16–19). Brook's community of theatrical collaborators, clearly centred around himself as the binding and driving force, but reaching outwards constantly in its search for renewal and communication, represents a possible achievement of Copeau's own aspirations for his experiments in Paris and Pernand-Vergelesses.

Jean Vilar (1912–1971) was a director, actor, and theatrical manager, and founder of the Festival d'Avignon and the Théâtre National Populaire. He was a friend of Charles Dullin who was an important influence on his work as an actor and as a director. His work reflects some of Copeau's moral integrity, as well as his respect for simple staging and minimal use of props. Like Copeau he emphasised the actor's economy of expression, through voice and through movement, and respected the centrality of the text. Strongly committed to a vision of high-quality popular theatre, he was an important figure in the democratisation of post-war French theatre. He also taught for a period at the École Jacques Lecoq.

Ariane Mnouchkine (1939–), the director of **Théâtre du Soleil** since its beginnings in 1964, has cited Copeau as a central influence on her work and her process and practices. Théâtre du Soleil's early ambition was the creation of a theatre which was both popular and political. In this respect their work can be seen as a part of the development of a popular theatre movement in France after the Second World War which drew from Copeau's early work and ideas. Equally their investigation of collective creation and civic responsibility, their 'prioritisation of the actor' and their emphasis on 'the discipline of mask work as corporeal and imaginal preparation' (Williams 1999: xiii), all reflect the profound influence of Copeau. Théâtre du Soleil's 'retreat' to the Cartoucherie de Vincennes, the former arsenal of the Chateau de Vincennes, whilst clearly not as dramatically rural as the Copiaus' retreat to Pernand-Vergelesses, suggests a similar commitment to theatre as an activity where work, training, performance and community are combined, and to an environment which restricts the intrusion of some of the more strident urban influences of Paris. Mnouchkine was a student at the École Jacques Lecoq from 1966 to 1967, and without doubt her time at the school gave flesh to Copeau's influence, representing as it does a line of practice from Copeau to Dasté to Lecoq. Further, by the early 1970s, Copeau's *Appels* (the first volume of *Les Registres*) had been published as a collected edition in Paris, allowing Mnouchkine and the company access to Copeau's own writings – his passionate belief in the value and importance of improvisation, and his commitment to the creation of an improvised comedy, a new *commedia dell'arte* for the new century. These ideas provided important inspiration for Théâtre du Soleil's 1975 production, *L'Age d'Or (The Golden Age)*. Like Copeau, the search was not for an historical reconstruction, but for a 'new improvised comedy' using 'contemporary types and subjects' (Copeau 1990: 153). Just as Copeau looked for inspiration to the classical theatre of Europe and the Far East, creating his own vision of theatre from a rich amalgam of experience gained through an open and generous engagement with the theatre texts of the past, so too Mnouchkine has brought a new, physical vitality and energy to productions of classical theatre texts, using these explorations to invigorate and inform her work on new texts and devised material. For Mnouchkine, Copeau represented a source of 'extraordinary things' (Williams 1999: 56), at least as important in the development of a theoretical understanding of her work as Brecht or Meyerhold, Artaud or **Zeami**.

Zeami (c. 1363–1443) was an actor, playwright and writer on the art of theatre in medieval Japan, largely credited with refining Japanese Nōh Theatre into a great form of world theatre. His writings focus on the achievement of grace and strength in acting.

Footsbarn was formed in 1970 by Oliver Foot and Jon-Paul Cook, with the aim of touring Cornwall with group-devised shows which celebrated the myths and legends of the region. The parallels between Footsbarn's work and the principles and practices of Jacques Copeau are evidenced 'in the desire to keep theatre presentations as simple, popular and accessible as possible' (Kilby 2005). Footsbarn has a commitment to creating theatre which is simple, celebratory, and exuberant. Their work involves improvisation and energy, and a playful attitude to their source material. Like Les Copiaus, they quickly became a self-sufficient community with strong social ties binding the group off-stage. After difficulties with funding the company left Cornwall in 1981 and embarked on a world tour, eventually settling in Maillet in France, where they are now based. Several members of the company have trained with Jacques Lecoq, and although the company makes no formal acknowledgement of Copeau's influence, his guiding spirit is evident in much of what they do and have achieved.

CONCLUSION

Copeau resolutely sought to renew the art of theatre throughout his life, yet he was not a modernist nor a revolutionary. His natural inclinations were both experimental and conservative. He was uncomfortable with a paradigm of progress which insisted on the replacement of old truths with new, for him progress was a process of renewal and rediscovery: 'There is in art a renewing of internal forces which is accomplished . . . through a periodic return to the original source' (Copeau in Kusler

1979: 4). Throughout his work we can detect a constant search for underlying truth, an almost archaeological passion for removing accumulated layers of theatrical silt and accretion to reveal the original dramatic source in its original colours: 'I am seeking to bring works closer to the "true tradition" by freeing them from the contributions loaded on them for three centuries by the official actors. The important tradition is the original one' (Copeau 1990: 145). Peeling away the layers of the actor's habits and clichés was the interior, psychological equivalent of Copeau's directorial approach to the script. For Copeau, it was only at this basic level of naked exposure to the play that real invention and genuine theatrical communication could begin.

At the heart of such a search is a belief in the value of the original. In returning to 'original' techniques and simple stage designs it was not Copeau's intention to produce plays in ways which were historically accurate – but rather to re-connect with what he understood as the original forces which drove these plays in performance. He believed that the inner energies of the play could be best released by placing the play at the centre of the rehearsal activity and encouraging the actors to let it take them over, rather than the other way round. This may be nothing more than a trick of the mind, but its effect was to facilitate an energised and self-less acting style and a more flexible and inquisitive approach to directing. The universalism which informs this work – a belief in an essential core to human nature, unchanging over time – is now out of tune with contemporary concerns to acknowledge diversity and difference. The tensions between contemporary theory and practices based on concepts of the 'natural' and 'neutral' body have been explored in detail elsewhere (Evans 2002), however whilst remaining critical of Copeau's universalism we can also recognise the socio-cultural and historical context which shaped it. His belief in some form of shared humanity and in its spiritual worth marks a significant position of resistance to the harsh delineations of difference promoted and imposed by German Nazism. Furthermore, his insistence on the paring away of the actor's habits and tricks reveals his commitment to a challenging and rigorous form of reflective practice for the actor. For the student of acting in the early twenty-first century, Copeau's ultimate legacy can be seen then as these core themes of openness, self-knowledge, communion, and sincerity; all linked through a process of training which in a significantly modern sense seeks to unite brain, body and emotions through a fundamental examination of their interconnectedness.

BIBLIOGRAPHY

Added, Serge (1996) 'Jacques Copeau and "Popular Theatre" in Vichy France', in Günter Berghaus (ed.) *Fascism and Theatre: Comparative Studies on the Aesthetics and Politics of Performance in Europe, 1925–1945*, Oxford: Berghahn Books, 247–59.

Anders, France (1959) *Jacques Copeau et le Cartel des Quatre*, Paris: A. G. Nizet.

Auslander, Philip (1997) *From Acting to Performance: Essays in Modernism and Postmodernism*, London: Routledge.

Bablet, Denis (1981) *The Theatre of Edward Gordon Craig*, London: Eyre Methuen.

Balance, J. [Edward Gordon Craig] (1908) 'A Note on Masks', *The Mask*, 1, 11.

Barker, Clive (1977) *Theatre Games: a New Approach to Drama Training*, London: Eyre Methuen.

Barrault, Jean-Louis (1951) *Reflections on the Theatre*, trans. Barbara Wall, London: Rockliff.

—— (1961) *The Theatre of Jean-Louis Barrault*, trans. Joseph Chiari, New York: Hill & Wang.

Benedetti, Jean (1988) *Stanislavski: a Biography*, London: Methuen.

Bentley, Eric (1950) 'Copeau and the Chimera', *Theatre Arts*, January, 34: 1, 48–51.

Bradby, David (1984) *Modern French Drama: 1940–1980*, Cambridge: Cambridge University Press.

Bradby, David and McCormick, John (1978) *People's Theatre*, London: Croom Helm.

Bradby, David and Williams, David (1988) *Directors' Theatre*, Basingstoke: Macmillan.

Bradby, David and Delgado, Maria (2002) *The Paris Jigsaw: Internationalism and the City's Stages*, Manchester: Manchester University Press.

Callery, Dymphna (2001) *Through the Body: a Practical Guide to Physical Theatre*, London: Nick Hern Books.

Carter, Huntley (1925) *The New Spirit in the European Theatre 1914–1924: a Comparative Study of Changes Effected by the War and Revolution*, London: Ernest Benn.

Christout, Marie-Françoise, Guibert, Noëlle and Pauly, Danièle (1993) *Théâtre du Vieux-Colombier: 1913–1993*, Paris: NORMA.

Clurman, Harold (1945) *The Fervent Years*, New York: Alfred A. Knopf.

Cole, Toby and Chinoy, Helen Krich (eds) (1970) *Actors on Acting: the Theories, Techniques, and Practices of the World's Greatest Actors, Told in Their Own Words*, New York: Three Rivers Press.

Copeau, Jacques (1931) *Souvenirs du Vieux-Colombier*, Paris: Nouvelles Editions.

—— (1941) *Le Théâtre Populaire*, Paris: Presses Universitaires de France.

—— (1963) 'Visites à Gordon Craig, Jaques-Dalcroze et Adolphe Appia', *Revue d'histoire du Théâtre*, 15ème année, December, 357–67.

—— (1967) 'An Essay of Dramatic Renovation: the Théâtre of the Vieux-Colombier', trans. Richard Hiatt, *Educational Theatre Journal*, Part 4, 447–54.

—— (1974) *Registres: Appels*, ed. Marie-Hélène Dasté and Suzanne Maistre Saint-Denis, Paris: Gallimard.

—— (1976) *Registres II: Molière*, ed. André Cabanis, Paris: Gallimard.

—— (1979) *Registres III: Les Registres du Vieux-Colombier premiere partie*, ed. Marie-Hélène Dasté and Suzanne Maistre Saint-Denis, Paris: Gallimard.

—— (1984) *Registres IV: Les Registres du Vieux-Colombier deuxième partie, America*, ed. Marie-Hélène Dasté and Suzanne Maistre Saint-Denis, Paris: Gallimard.

—— (1990) *Copeau: Texts on Theatre*, trans. and ed. John Rudlin and Norman Paul, London: Routledge.

—— (1993) *Registres V: Les Registres du Vieux-Colombier troisième partie, 1919–1924*, ed. Suzanne Maistre Saint-Denis, Marie-Hélène Dasté, Norman Paul, Clément Borgal and Maurice Jacquemont, Paris: Gallimard.

—— (2000) *Registres VI: L'École du Vieux-Colombier*, ed. Claude Sicard, Paris: Gallimard.

Darwin, Charles (1872) *The Expression of the Emotions in Man and Animals*, London.

Decroux, Etienne (1985) 'Words on Mime', trans. Mark Piper, *Mime Journal: Words on Mime*, Claremont, CA: Pamona College.

Doisy, Marcel (1954) *Jacques Copeau*, Paris: Le Cercle du Livre.

Donahue, Thomas (1991) 'Mnouchkine, Vilar and Copeau: Popular Theater and Paradox', *Modern Language Studies*, 21: 4, 31–42.

—— (1998) 'Improvisation and the Mask at the École du Vieux-Colombier: the Case of Suzanne Bing', *Maske Und Korthurn*, 44: 1–2, 61–72.

Dorcy, Jean (1961) *The Mime*, trans. Robert Speller, Jr. and Pierre de Fontnouvelle, New York: Robert Speller.

Dukes, Ashley (1931) 'The English Scene', *Theatre Arts Monthly*, September, XV: 9, 715–19.

—— (1935) 'The Scene in Europe: Theatre and School', *Theatre Arts Monthly*, April, XIX: 4, 259–63.

Eldredge, Sears (1979) 'Jacques Copeau and the Mask in Actor Training', *Mime, Mask, and Marionette*, 2, 3–4, 1979–1980.

Eldredge, Sears (1996) *Mask Improvisation for Actor Training and Performance: the Compelling Image*, Evanston, IL: Northwestern University Press.

Eldredge, Sears and Huston, Hollis (1995) 'Actor Training in the Neutral Mask', in Philip Zarrilli (ed.) *Acting (Re)Considered: Theories and Practices*, London and New York: Routledge.

Evans, Mark (2002) 'Movement Training for the English Actor in the Twentieth Century: Conceptual Structures and Body Learning', unpublished PhD thesis, Coventry University.

Feinsod, Arthur (1992) *The Simple Stage: Its Origins in the Modern American Theatre*, New York: Greenwood Press.

Felner, Mira (1985) *Apostles of Silence: the Modern French Mimes*, London: Associated University Presses.

Frank, Waldo (1925) 'Copeau Begins Again', *Theatre Arts Monthly*, 9, September.

Frost, Anthony and Yarrow, Ralph. (1990) *Improvisation in Drama*, Basingstoke: Macmillan.

Ghéon, Henri (1961) *The Art of the Theatre*, trans. Adele Fiske, New York: Hill & Wang.

Gignoux, Hubert (1984) *Histoire d'une Famille Théâtrale: Jacques Copeau – Léon Chancerel, Les Comédiens-Routiers, La Décentralisation dramatique*, Lausanne: Éditions de l'Aire.

Gontard, Denis (ed.) (1974) *Le Journal de Bord des Copiaus 1924–1929*, Paris: Seghers.

Guicharnaud, Jacques (1967) *Modern French Theatre: from Giraudoux to Genet*, New Haven, CT: Yale University Press.

Harrop, John. (1971) '"A Constructive Promise": Jacques Copeau in New York, 1917–1919', *Theatre Survey*, November, XII: 2, 104–18.

Hayman, Ronald (1977) *Artaud and After*, Oxford: Oxford University Press.

Hébert, Georges (1949) *L'Éducation physique par la méthode naturelle*, 10 vols, Paris: Librarie Vuibert.

Hobson, Harold (1978) *French Theatre Since 1830*, London: John Calder.

Innes, Christopher (1993) *Avant Garde Theatre: 1892–1992*, London: Routledge.

Jaques-Dalcroze, Emile (1906) *Méthode Jaques-Dalcroze: Pour le dévèloppement de l'instinct rythmiques, du sens auditif et du sentiment tonal, en 5 parties*, Neuchâtel: Sandoz, Jobin & Cie.

—— (1913) *The Eurhythmics of Jaques-Dalcroze*, introduced by Prof. M. E. Sadler, Boston, MA: Small Maynard.

Johnstone, Keith (1981) *Impro: Improvisation and the Theatre*, London: Eyre Methuen.

Kilby, John (2005) Personal email to author (8 April).

Knapp, Bettina (1988) *The Reign of the Theatrical Director: French Theatre: 1887–1924*, Albany, NY: Whitston.

Kurtz, Maurice (1999) *Jacques Copeau: the Biography of a Theatre*, Carbonda, CO: Southern Illinois University Press.

Kusler, Barbara Leigh (1974) 'Jacques Copeau's Theatre School: l'École du Vieux-Colombier, 1920–1929', unpublished PhD thesis, University of Wisconsin.

Kusler, Barbara Leigh (1979) 'Jacques Copeau's School for Actors: Commemorating the Centennial of the Birth of Jacques Copeau', *Mime Journal: Numbers Nine and Ten*, Claremont, CA: Pamona College.

Leabhart, Thomas (1989) *Modern and Postmodern Mime*, Basingstoke: Macmillan.

Leabhart, Thomas (1995) 'The Mask as Shamanic Tool in the Theatre Training of Jacques Copeau', *Mime Journal: Incorporated Knowledge*, Claremont, CA: Pamona College, 82–113.

Leabhart, Thomas (2004) 'Jacques Copeau, Etienne Decroux, and the "Flower of Noh"', *New Theatre Quarterly*, November, XX: 4, 315–30.

Lecoq, Jacques (ed.) (1987) *Le Théâtre du Geste: Mimes et Acteurs*, Paris: Bordas.

Merlin, Bella (2003) *Konstantin Stanislavsky*, London: Routledge.

Meyerhold, Vsevolod (1981) *Meyerhold on Theatre*, trans. and ed. Edward Braun, London: Eyre Methuen.

Mignon, Paul-Louis (1993) *Jacques Copeau ou le mythe du Vieux-Colombier: Biographie*, Paris: Julliard.

Miller, Anna Irene (1931) *The Independent Theatre in Europe: 1887 to the Present*, New York: Benjamin Blom.

Milling, Jane and Ley, Graham (2001) *Modern Theories of Performance*, Basingstoke: Palgrave.

Mingalon, Jean-Louis (1999) 'An Interview with Marie-Hélène Dasté', *Mime Journal: Transmissions*, 11–27.

Molière (1951) *Les Fourberies de Scapin – mise en scène et commentaries de Jacques Copeau*, Paris: Éditions du Seuil.

Molière (1962) *The Miser and other plays*, trans. John Wood, Harmondsworth: Penguin.

Murray, Simon (2003) *Jacques Lecoq*, London: Routledge.

Paul, Norman (1977) 'Jacques Copeau, Drama Critic', *Theatre Research International*, May, II : 3, 221–9.

Paul, Norman (1979) *Bibliographie Jacques Copeau*, Paris: Société les Belles Lettres.

Paul, Norman (1987) Review of 'Jacques Copeau' by John Rudlin, *Modern Drama*, December, 30: 4, 582–3.

Rogers, Clark (1966) 'The Influence of Dalcroze Eurhythmics in the Contemporary Theatre', unpublished PhD Thesis, University of Wisconsin.

Rogers, Clark (1969) 'Appia's Theory of Acting: Eurhythmics for the Stage', E. T. Kirby (ed.) *Total Theatre: A Critical Anthology*, New York: Dutton.

Rudlin, John (1986) *Jacques Copeau*, Cambridge: Cambridge University Press.

Rudlin, John (1996) 'Play's the Thing', *Mime Journal: Theatre and Sport*, Claremont, CA: Pamona College, 17–29.

Rudlin, John (2000) 'Jacques Copeau: the Quest for Sincerity', Alison Hodge (ed.) *Twentieth Century Actor Training*, London: Routledge, 55–78.

Ruffini, Franco (1995) 'Mime, the Actor, Action: the Way of Boxing', *Mime Journal: Incorporated Knowledge*, Claremont, CA: Pamona College, 54–69.

Saint-Denis, Michel (1960) *Theatre: the Rediscovery of Style*, London: Heinemann.

Saint-Denis, Michel (1967) 'Stanislavski and Shakespeare', trans. Simone Sanzenbach, in Erika Munk (ed.) *Stanislavski and America: 'The Method' and Its Influence on the American Theatre*, Greenwich, CN: Fawcett Premier.

Saint-Denis, Michel (1982) *Training for the Theatre: Premises and Promises*, London: Heinemann.

Sorell, Walter (1973) *The Other Face: the Mask in the Arts*, Indianapolis, IN: Bobbs-Merrill.

Spector, Irwin (1990) *Rhythm and Life: the Work of Emile Jaques-Dalcroze*, Stuyvesant, NY: Pendragon Press.

Taylor, Graham (1999) 'François Delsarte: a Codification of Nineteenth-Century Acting', *Theatre Research International*, 24: 1, 71–81.

Volbach, Walter (1965) 'Jacques Copeau, Appia's Finest Disciple', *Educational Theatre Journal*, December.

Waley, Arthur (ed. and trans.) (1976) *The Nō Plays of Japan*, Ruland, VT: Charles E. Tuttle.

Ward, Nigel (1996) '"Théâtre Populaire": Ideology and Tradition in French Popular Theatre', in Ros Merkin (ed.) (1996) *Popular Theatres?: Papers from the Popular Theatre Conference, Liverpool John Moores University, 1994*, Liverpool: Liverpool John Moores University, 172–82.

Williams, David (ed.) *Collaborative Theatre: the Théâtre du Soleil Sourcebook*, London: Routledge.

ARCHIVE MATERIAL

'French Theatre du Vieux-Colombier', programme for New York season, 1917–1918. (Fonds Copeau – Bibliothèque nationale de France, Paris).

OTHER RESOURCES

For those interested in further study there is a substantial archive of material on Copeau's life and work available in the Copeau Archives (or *Fonds Copeau*) at the Bibliothèque nationale de France in Paris. An archive of material which previously belonged to John Ruldin is available at the Templeman Library of the University of Kent.

WEBSITES

Bibliothèque nationale de France, Paris. Online, available: http://www.bnf.fr (20 September 2005).

Footsbarn, Maillet. Online, available: http://footsbarn.com (20 September 2005).

Jacques Copeau Archive, *Templeman Library of the University of Kent*, Canterbury. Online, available: http://library.kent.ac.uk/library/special/html/specoll/COPEAU3.HTM (20 September 2005).

Théâtre du Soleil, Paris. Online, available: http://www.theatre-du-soleil.fr (20 September 2005).

Théâtre du Vieux-Colombier, Paris. Online, available: http://vieux.colombier.free.fr (20 September 2005).

INDEX

Theatre Histories:
An Introduction

Edited by Philip B. Zarrilli, Bruce McConachie, Gary Jay Williams and Carol Fisher Sorgenfrei

'This book will significantly change theatre education'
Janelle Reinelt, *University of California, Irvine*

Theatre Histories: An Introduction is a radically new way of looking at both the way history is written and the way we understand performance.

The authors provide beginning students and teachers with a clear, exciting journey through centuries of European, North and South American, African and Asian forms of theatre and performance.

Challenging the standard format of one-volume theatre history texts, they help the reader think critically about this vibrant field through fascinating yet plain-speaking essays and case studies.

Among the topics covered are:

- representation and human expression
- interpretation and critical approaches
- historical method and sources
- communication technologies
- colonization
- oral and literate cultures
- popular, sacred and elite forms of performance.

Keeping performance and culture very much centre stage, *Theatre Histories: An Introduction* is compatible with standard play anthologies, full of insightful pedagogical apparatus, and comes accompanied by web site resources.

ISBN10: 0–415–22727–5 (hbk)
ISBN10: 0–415–22728–3 (pbk)

ISBN13: 978–0–415–22727–8 (hbk)
ISBN13: 978–0–415–22728–5 (pbk)

Available at all good bookshops
For ordering and further information please visit:
www.routledge.com

Related titles from Routledge

The Routledge Companion to Theatre and Performance

Edited by Paul Allain and Jen Harvie

What is theatre? What is performance? What are their connections and differences? What events, people, practices and ideas have shaped theatre and performance in the twentieth century, and, importantly, where are they heading next?

Proposing answers to these big questions, *The Routledge Companion to Theatre and Performance* provides an informative and engaging introduction to the significant people, events, concepts and practices that have defined the complementary fields of theatre and performance studies.

Including over 120 entries in three easy-to-use, alphabetical sections, this fascinating text presents a wide range of individuals and topics, from performance artist Marina Abramovic, to directors Vsevolod Meyerhold and Robert Wilson, The Living Theatre's *Paradise Now*, *the haka*, multimedia performance, political protest and visual theatre.

With each entry containing crucial historical and contextual information, extensive cross-referencing, detailed analysis, and an annotated bibliography, *The Routledge Companion to Theatre and Performance* is undoubtedly a perfect reference guide for the keen student and passionate theatre-goer alike.

ISBN10: 0–415–25720–4 (hbk)
ISBN10: 0–415–25721–2 (pbk)

Available at all good bookshops
For ordering and further information please visit:
www.routledge.com

Related titles from Routledge

Performance Studies:
An Introduction
2nd Edition
Richard Schechner

Praise for the first edition:
'An appropriately broad-ranging, challenging, and provocative introduction, equally important for practicing artists as for students and scholars of the performing arts.'

Phillip Zarrilli, *University of Exeter*

Fully revised and updated in light of recent world events, this important new edition of a key introductory textbook by a prime mover in the field provides a lively and accessible overview of the full range of performance.

Performance Studies includes discussion of the performing arts and popular entertainments, rituals, play and games as well as the performances of everyday life. Supporting examples and ideas are drawn from the performing arts, anthropology, post-structuralism, ritual theory, ethology, philosophy and aesthetics.

The text has been fully revised, with input from leading teachers and trialled with students. User-friendly, with a special text design, it also includes:

- new examples, biographies, source material and photographs
- numerous extracts from primary sources giving alternative voices and viewpoints
- biographies of key thinkers
- activities to stimulate fieldwork, classroom exercises and discussion
- key readings for each chapter
- twenty line drawings and 202 photographs drawn from private and public collections around the world.

For undergraduates at all levels and beginning graduate students in performance studies, theatre, performing arts and cultural studies, this is the must-have book in the field.

ISBN10: 0–415–37245–3 (hbk)
ISBN10: 0–415–37246–1 (pbk)

Available at all good bookshops
For ordering and further information please visit:
www.routledge.com

Related titles from Routledge

The Performance Studies Reader

Edited by Henry Bial

'A collection of this type has been needed for a long time.'
Sally Harrison-Pepper, *Miami University*

'Clearly an important collection of essays that will provide an excellent resource for levels II and III specialist courses.'
Nick Kaye, *Exeter University*

The Performance Studies Reader is a lively and much-needed anthology of critical writings on the burgeoning discipline of performance studies. It provides an overview of the full range of performance theory for undergraduates at all levels, and beginning graduate students in performance studies, theatre, performing arts and cultural studies.

The collection is designed as a companion to Richard Schechner's popular *Performance Studies: An Introduction* but is also ideal as a stand-alone text. Henry Bial collects together key critical pieces from the field, referred to as 'suggested readings' in *Performance Studies: An Introduction*. He also broadens the discussion with additional selections. Featuring contributions from major scholars and artists such as Richard Schechner, Eugenio Barba, Marvin Carlson, Judith Butler, Jon McKenzie, Homi K. Bhabha, Eve Kosofsky Sedgwick and Jerzy Grotowski, this important collection offers a wide-ranging introduction to the main areas of study.

ISBN10: 0–415–30240–4 (hbk)
ISBN10: 0–415–30241–2 (pbk)

Available at all good bookshops
For ordering and further information please visit:
www.routledge.com